WHAT PEOPLE ARE SAYING...

Jacob's Story, detailing the story of Jakob Schleicher, is a well-written detailed account of his personal and professional journey. His amazing story unfolds in Germany, later emigrating to America where he started the first successful factory building American gas engines, continuing onward with a Philadelphia-based confectionary company. This must-read book from author/historian Erik Varon, magically captures the ups and downs of a creative 19th century entrepreneur experiencing the American Dream.

—Wayne Grenning, Chief Engineer,
Coolspring Power Museum

"Anyone who has been an immigrant, has known an immigrant, or who has descended from an immigrant will find a great deal to ponder in Jakob's Story and the American Dream. Erik Varon weaves a compelling story of how Jakob Schleicher, a Belgian-born youth of German ancestry, was transformed into James Schleicher, an American businessman who dreamed of a world in which art and culture would triumph over national division."

—Robert Wojtowicz, Ph.D., Dean of the Graduate School
and Professor of Art History, Old Dominion University

Jakob's Story and the American Dream

Jakob's Story and the American Dream

by Erik Varon

Maracaibo Publishing
GLENDORA, CALIFORNIA

© 2017 by Erik Varon. All rights reserved

All rights reserved. No part of this publication may be reproduced, distributed or transmitted in any form or by any means, including photocopying, recording, or other electronic or mechanical methods, without the prior written permission of the publisher, except in the case of brief quotations embodied in critical reviews and certain other noncommercial uses permitted by copyright law. For permission requests, write to the publisher, with the subject line "Attention: Permissions Coordinator," at the email address below.

Maracaibo Publishing
sales@maracaibopublishing.com
jakobsstory.com

Book midwife, final edit, cover and interior layout design:
Ruth Schwartz, TheWonderlady.com

Front cover designed by Erik Varon and Ruth Schwartz.
Immigration document courtesy Ancestry.com.
Photo of Jakob Schleicher courtesy Rosalind Chadwick-Garrigle and Susan Mallaney.

Ordering Information:
Quantity sales. Special discounts are available on quantity purchases by corporations, associations, and others. For details, contact the "Special Sales Department" at the address above.

JAKOB'S STORY/ Erik Varon. — 1st ed.
ISBN 978-0-9990559-0-8 paperback
ISBN 978-0-9990559-1-5 ebook
Library of Congress Control Number: 2017908419

Dedication

My Dear Agnes: I am blessed to have a wife who is as loving and giving as you. In allowing me the opportunity to write this story and sacrificing the irreplaceable gift of your time, you have given me the chance to live a portion of my American Dream. Quoting Cowboy Kent Rollins, I am reminded that,
"A man is only as strong as the woman who holds him."

*Thank you for holding me, loving me
and supporting me in my endeavor.*

*Your husband,
-Erik*

The unexamined life is not worth living.

—Socrates

ACKNOWLEDGMENTS

This American story could not have been told without the help of the following people. Beginning with my talented editor, Susan Herman; a very special thank you for gently guiding this novice author through the sometimes foggy and confusing forest of storytelling.

Thank you and special recognition to the late William Garrigle. William, his wife, Rosalind and their daughter, Susan Mallaney — all three have been so wonderfully helpful, supportive and cooperative. They entrusted me with access to their family photos and other documents I needed to accurately tell Jakob's story.

To Steve Forster: your candid critique inspired and personally challenged me to keep researching and to dig deeper within myself in order to tell a more detailed story.

To Wayne Grenning: Wayne, your expertise in the engine field, your willingness to share your photos, articles, interviews and even an excerpt from your manuscript has been nothing short of amazing. What rich resources these are. I could not have crafted this account without you! Thank you, my friend.

To Tilar Mazzeo: without you sharing your expertise and insight into the proper ways of storytelling this narrative would never have become possible.

To Robert Wojtowicz and Aggie: both of you took the time to honestly critique and appraise the manuscript. Without the valuable input from each of you, I would not have this final edition.

These remaining names and organizations have also provided crucial information. It's been a team effort. Thank you!

Chris Bellanger, Sara Border, Lucas R. Clawson, Phil Cohen, Patrick Connelly, Christopher Damiani, Janina Decker, Dana Dorman, Linda Gross, Joel Havens, Frank Heidermanns, Ralf

Krüger, Hermann Langen, Klaus Lüdtke, Jouni Filip Maho, Jane McGuinness, Scott McGurk, Kenneth Milano, Scott Mosley, Joe Murphy, Wade V. Myers, Erika Piola, Greg Plunges, Bill Roorbach, Ruth Schwartz, Lynsey Sczechowicz, Nancy Shawcross, Jonathan R. Stayer, George Tselos, Dietmar Voss, Jacinda Williams, Ed Youngblood, Ancestry.com, the British Library, California State Polytechnic University of Pomona, Camden County Historical Society, Chicago History Museum, Coolspring Power Museum, Deutz AG, Glendora Public Library, Great War Primary Document Archives (GWPDA.org), Hagley Museum, Harvard Library, Historical Society of Pennsylvania, Historical Society of the United States District Court for the District of New Jersey, Los Angeles Public Library, Mount Vernon Cemetery, National Archives at New York City, National Parks Service, and the Ohio State University Library.

TABLE OF CONTENTS

Introduction 1
1: A Foreign Time and Place 7
2: Reminiscences of an Old Man 13
3: A European Boyhood 23
4: Liberty Enlightening the World 33
5: The Otto-Langen Experiment 47
6: Jakob's American Dream Begins 59
7: The Centennial Exhibition of 1876 69
8: Schleicher, Schumm & Company 81
9: A Twist of Fate 97
10: Industrialism, Progressivism and a Brief Retirement 107
11: The Philadelphia Caramel Company 117
12: The Three Uninvited Guests 127
13: The Great War 137
14: The Lawsuit 149
15: Jakob's Declining Years 159
16: The Clock Winds Down 171
17: Lewis Mumford's Closing Thoughts 183
Selected Bibliography 195
About the Author 205

Introduction

For over one hundred and fifty years the United States of America has provided each of its citizens, regardless of their gender, ethnicity, place of origin, or religious belief, the opportunity to do more than just succeed; this country has given each person the chance to excel. Not limited to those who are affluent, wealthy or come from royalty, the opportunity America provides is instead based on each individual's own abilities, allowing everyone a fair and equal chance to become a doctor, politician, professional athlete or take on any number of other professions. America has become known as the land where all have a chance to make a better, richer and more abundant life for themselves. This opportunity is what Samuel Francis Smith referred to in 1831 when he crafted the patriotic song "My Country 'Tis of Thee." Invoking the freedom that the founding fathers sought, this song lauds America as being a "Sweet Land of Liberty." Freedom, combined with the equal opportunity to achieve, is often referred to as "the American Dream." Without the American Dream, even individuals with many natural gifts — such as W.E.B. Du Bois, Henry Ford,

Thomas Edison and Charlie Chaplin—would never have left their distinct mark in history. They, along with countless others, likely would have remained unknown had they not been given the chance to pursue their dreams.

All generations of Americans have dreamt of finding success. Each generation has many models of self-reliance and determination among its members: pioneers and problem-solvers who inspire others to dream. From the founding fathers' desire for independence, to the early settlers who ventured west, the people of the United States have always been forward thinkers who desire to broaden their horizons. This spirit of exploration lent momentum to innovators/heroes like the Wright Brothers as they reached for the skies, and risk-takers like Neil Armstrong, as he stepped foot on the moon.

As a result of the Dream, the United States of America has become more than just a country or a geographic location on a map. *America* is instead an idea that embodies the human spirit of creativity, innovation and entrepreneurship. But along with this opportunity that America provides, there is another attribute that has made America the greatest nation on earth. As retired four-star General Colin Powell once remarked, "The defining strength of America is our people." It is therefore both the opportunity and the people who have come to define this country. From one generation to the next, the act of offering someone else an opportunity is a mark of pride among Americans for their country's greatness.

In some respects, the American Dream is not limited to those of us living in this country. Indeed, every year the Dream draws millions of immigrants from all corners of the globe to this country seeking the same hope, fulfillment and abundance citizens sometimes take for granted. While the American Dream has never promised anyone an automatic right to a richer, fuller

JAKOB'S STORY AND THE AMERICAN DREAM

or happier life, everyone in America is given the same platform and opportunity to find joy--no matter what we wish to pursue in our lives. For many who live elsewhere, American society and its way of life is so appealing that they consider risking certain danger to migrate to this country.

Simultaneously, this country has welcomed immigrants with their creative ideas to help build a better and more advanced America for all. Some of these notable immigrants include Alexander Graham Bell, Gugliemo Marconi (inventor of the radiola) and Albert Einstein. Each of these innovators played a unique part in shaping the society we now live in. Had it not been for the opportunities these individuals were given and the success each of them achieved, we would not have the modern amenities we now use on a daily basis.

Jakob Schleicher was an immigrant who came to the United States in 1876. He too helped shape America during this country's Industrial Era, though his story is not well known. At the time of his arrival, America relied heavily on the steam engine, with the locomotive and steam ship being the primary ways of traveling long distances. But as a result of the ingenuity of two Germans, Nicholas Otto and his business partner, Eugen Langen, the steam engine faced a new competitor: the gas-powered engine. Jakob Schleicher played an important role in the development of this new technology. He introduced the first internal combustion (gas-powered) engine to America in 1876. It was for this purpose that Jakob traveled to America.

Jakob's Story and the American Dream is a literary non-fiction account that explores Jakob Schleicher's life story, his journey to America and his experience of living the American Dream. In an effort to fully capture the challenges he experienced as an immigrant pursuing the American Dream, this story also delves into the many moving parts occurring within the United States during the late nineteenth century and the early twentieth century.

Beginning with his days of being raised in the old country of Belgium, follow along as Jakob became one of the many entrepreneurs who seized the opportunity to display their creativity and new ideas to the American public, arriving in America just in time to take part in the six-month Great Centennial Exhibition of 1876. Hosted in Philadelphia, the exhibition not only celebrated America's 100th anniversary of the signing of the Declaration of Independence, it also highlighted the technological advancements that had been made in the world over the past one hundred years. Traveling thousands of miles from home, this exhibition marked the beginning of a successful business venture in America for Jakob Schleicher.

As any business owner today will avow, change is the only constant. At the turn of the twentieth century, as technology advanced, Schleicher decided to end his first business venture and repurpose himself in a new field. Initially he would find the same level of success in marketing confections as he originally had found in the production of gas-powered engines.

Then, when his beloved Germany looked to expand its empire and its influence in Europe, the Great European War (World War I), set off a chain of events around the world. Jakob, with his unpopular loyalties to the Fatherland, was not untouched. In fact, his world collapsed.

So, why tell Jakob's story? If his collaboration on the gas engine and success in the candy industry weren't enough on their own to make him a household name, why bother?

Because Jakob Schleicher's story, with all of its twists and turns, is our story. Early in the twenty-first century we now find our society searching for the "what now?". Just as industrialization brought about advancements in technology and transportation, social roles (such as male dominance in lawmaking, business ownership, and most everything else) were rapidly changing. Likewise today, social, economic and world issues influence an entire generation — including its little-known innovators. They, like Jakob Schleicher might launch and excel in one moment, but fail the next. It is important to note that freedom to fail is the other side of the opportunity coin, and one's social capital is a thing to be managed, as carefully or more carefully than, say, one's inventory, property, or skill bank.

This account not only narrates Jakob Schleicher's life story, but in the end it will also illustrate the risks the American Dream presents. Is it worth pursuing the American Dream if achieving it doesn't look the way we thought it would? Were he alive today, Jakob Schleicher might say yes, it's worth it. He would probably argue that dreaming the Dream is part of what it means to be human. For it is in our humanness that we leave behind a lasting legacy.

This is the essence of his story.

CHAPTER 1

A Foreign Time and Place

The loneliest moment in someone's life is when they are watching their whole world fall apart, and all they can do is stare blankly.
— F. Scott Fitzgerald, *The Great Gatsby*

2:49 AM. Having gradually lost much of life's vigor over the past several years, Jakob Schleicher's gaunt, seventy-four-year-old body lay in bed. Jakob was wide awake, confused and conflicted. He had endured many restless and sleepless nights within these last few weeks as a result of recurring, troubling thoughts. Partially out of frustration, but also as a means of being productive, he quietly sat up in bed. Jakob still abided by two lessons he learned in his youth: time is precious; don't waste it. *Indeed, there is no second to be lost or wasted* was his adopted mantra. If he could not sleep, he simply would not waste a full hours' time lying awake in bed.

It was the winter of 1925. With his sunset years behind him and now drifting in his final stage in life, Jakob took a little longer to exit his bed and shuffle across his bedroom. As he slowly made his way from the room he rented, working his way down the hallway of this two-story, Victorian-style home, the creaking sound of the hardwood floors interrupted the early morning silence. So as not to disturb the landlord downstairs, Jakob slowed his pace and walked delicately toward his library.

Jakob's library was not a large room, perhaps ten feet by twelve feet, but it had become something special to him. Much like a sanctuary, it was a place where, over the past several weeks, he spent the majority of his days focusing on his favorite activities: reading his beloved literature, crafting poetry, and penning an assortment of other writings. More than just a retreat, his library was also where Jakob found solace and security in his unstable and scary world.

Knowledgeable, savvy and still sharp-witted a decade after his unexpected retirement, Jakob Schleicher spent a portion of each day reflecting on various subjects. While some days he spent time critically analyzing current events, lately he had begun spending increasing amounts of time nostalgically looking back on the most cherished events throughout his life.

Arriving in his library, Jakob quietly turned on the light and closed the door. Once inside, he powered on his battery-operated Atwater Kent radiola, with its many dials and corresponding horn speaker, was a portable, shoebox-sized unit. While its dark mahogany cabinet exhibited a clean and pristine appearance, it revealed something more. The high gloss and sheen was an outward symbol of Jakob's inward pride, as he always took utmost and meticulous care of his wares. Although he was only able to receive two stations on his radiola in his hometown of Merchantville, New Jersey, Jakob enjoyed with discriminating pleasure listening to the day's programming, no matter how minimal the selection.

Having warmed up, the radiola began to play music softly in the background, albeit with a scratchy and muffled quality. Momentarily pausing to look at the radiola, Jakob ran his hand across the top of the cabinet with a slow and gentle sweep. He then turned and walked to the nearby sofa where he seated himself.

Jakob's thoughts dwelled on various events that had taken place over the past six to eight years. In America, around the world, and even in his own life, dramatic changes seemed to have swept across every surface. After the tragedies that took place during the Great War (World War I), everyone seemed to discard old beliefs, old regimes and former ways of doing things in exchange for embracing a newer way of life.

By 1925 many long-held and cherished traditions had been broken or had morphed unrecognizably. American society no longer held itself to what Jakob felt were the proper Victorian standards of earlier years. In their modes of dress and even in the way they interacted with others, younger Americans were carrying themselves differently. To Jakob the flappers, for example, looked and acted in ways that were utterly unfamiliar and foreign, calling it their "artistic expression."

Dubbed flappers in reference to a young bird flapping its wings while learning how to fly, these young women, in style and attitude, had come to define an entire generation. To start, flappers exemplified the emergence of a "new, modern woman." With her bobbed hair, provocative dress and wild dancing, she was considered by many older people in society to be too brash and rebellious. *If this is what happens when young women start working and earning their own money, I'll have none of it,* Jakob scoffed.

Jakob was fully aware that every generation's standards and attitudes varied from its previous counterpart's. As a youth growing up in the old country of Belgium, he remembered how his parents once held strict, traditional values that he thought were too rigid and too old-fashioned. Still, one had to draw a line somewhere.

Another disturbing development had come about just a few months prior. In July 1925, John T. Scopes, a Tennessee teacher, was convicted in court of teaching evolution. The very idea that God could have created species of plants and animals that weren't perfect in the first place, that they had to undergo changes over time to become what one saw around one today—ridiculous! God wanted people to be the rational, thinking creatures we are today. Else why would God have created monkeys at all, if what He really wanted (millennia later, mind you) was humans? Rubbish. Having lived in America for fifty years, Jakob simply could not decipher these new standards of the day. What's more, he knew he was not alone in feeling as if he were a stranger who had traveled to a foreign time and place.

From his sofa Jakob's attention was drawn to a framed photo atop his desk. It was a picture of him and his wife. Staring at it, he thought back to a happier time and place—a time when he was younger, when he had a partner and the world was a less complicated place. With all of these social changes, he anxiously thought to himself that life was becoming more complex, confusing and scary. As his body slowed down, Jakob was feeling more and more out of place. Unlike earlier years when life had brought prosperity and happiness, Jakob now faced the challenges of old age with loneliness as his only companion.

JAKOB'S STORY AND THE AMERICAN DREAM

Retired for a number of years, Jakob rented a room located in the upper-middle class suburb of Merchantville from a pleasant, middle-aged German couple and their children. He and another tenant rented the two upstairs bedrooms. But with no real bond or deep connection with this family, and with his wife having passed away what seemed like a lifetime ago, emotionally Jakob lived alone. Finding himself with ample amounts of time and no one with whom to argue or commiserate over society's ills, he thought more and more of his past, where he had come from, what he had seen and experienced and what it all meant.

It was also during these years that Jakob was finding that the certainties of the Enlightenment—from his most cherished beliefs to his long-held core values—had seemingly become antiquated and outdated. Furthermore, if his morals and standards no longer had a place in the world, Jakob began to wonder what, if any importance *he* still had, and to whom?

Then, in an odd-feeling moment—experiencing what one might call a paradox—as he sat in his library on that early morning winter day, Jakob suddenly thought: *The world is changing, yes. It is, in fact, evolving. Everyone in it is on their own journey of discovery.* As the flappers, Prohibition and evolution itself were making the 1920s an age of extremes, Jakob realized that it was not such a stark contrast with the way life used to be. Rather, a more accurate description was that his life had gone full circle from an unfamiliar beginning, returning back to an unfamiliar ending. It was also at that moment that Jakob had a premonition that he had completed the circle of life. His life was approaching its end. As if preparing for a final exam, Jakob felt inclined to reexamine his life one last time, analyzing the various pieces of it and penning it into a memoir.

CHAPTER 2

Reminiscences of an Old Man

In many lives it is the beginnings that are most significant: the first steps, though seemingly effaced, leave their imprint on everything else that follows.
— **Lewis Mumford, American historian and literary critic**

Jakob slowly arose from the couch. As he made his way over to his desk he began to think of how he wanted to craft his memoir. What essential events did he want to include? How did he want to begin? And who was going to read it? He pondered these thoughts as he walked across the library toward his desk at the other end of the room.

Arriving at his desk he retrieved his old pair of pince-nez spectacles. By the mid-1920s this form of eyewear was out of style and no longer popular. But clipping them onto the bridge of his nose he thought to himself, *humbug to those who think these are too stuffy and too old-fashioned.* With his spectacles properly situated, Jakob placed a pad of paper on the desk and spent a few moments letting his mind wander back into the past. Still a bit unsure as to how he would craft this piece, he recalled that Aldous Huxley, a popular English writer, once wrote "Every man's memory is his private literature."

Soon his motivation and purpose became clear. He decided to write with the intention of helping someone, by passing on a bit of wisdom he learned along the way. As if it were yesterday, his memory quickly took him back seventy years. Jakob began his memoir by jotting down in chronological order those thoughts and memories that had made the biggest impression on his life. With an engineer's precision, Jakob neatly organized his memoir into seven sections: his early youth, a lesson in liberty and loyalty, a technological experiment he became a part of and his subsequent journey to America, the twentieth century marking the start of new beginnings, the war years, losing everything, and a few other miscellaneous thoughts. After about a half-hour of jotting down several pages of notes, he was ready to chronicle seventy-four years worth of private literature.

Adjacent to his desk was a small table with a typewriter. Taking his notes, Jakob slid over slightly and aligned himself in front of the typewriter. Making himself comfortable, he leaned forward slightly and began pecking.

> It is a question how far back recollections of our childhood can be traced reliably and how much of it is but part of elder people's tales from the past...

In 1905, some twenty years before this particular winter evening, renowned physiologist Sigmund Freud formed the opinion that most childhood memories are permanently lost as a result of "the remarkable amnesia of childhood." Freud, who was sometimes referred to as the father of psychoanalysis, believed that this phenomenon was perhaps a result of early human experiences not being encoded properly, or possibly due to the human brain still being in a developmental stage, such that rapid growth took precedence over memory storage until about the age of four. As a result, only the tiniest glimpses from an individual's earliest existence can be recalled without the aid of an older family member or relative who was present at particular events.

From the murky visions of his own childhood, Jakob recounted and documented his earliest memory. "Our earliest home which I can remember, being about four years old, was along New Street in Antwerp (Belgium)." He then provided a vague description of this early home: "It was a three-story residence with a porte-cochere on the left and a row of two windows on the right." Jakob acknowledged his inability to recall every detail of this home, noting that "Our homes furnish us a background against which but few images of the past will arise before our inner eye." Thinking of this home, he did manage to recount the following:

> I remember how on a wintery day with a hot coal fire in the iron-stove safely railed in, I was squatting on the floor on a bear skin, busy with picture books and toys while the mild rays of the sun were playing in my flaxen curls.

Jakob carried this descriptive and animated narration style throughout his memoir, as was fitting for someone of that era with an advanced education. His command of the English language was fluid and idiomatic.

The typewriter stopped for a moment as he paused to think about why these memories were so deeply impressed. To start, he reflected that recalling a cozy and warm environment from his childhood gave him a feeling of security and reassurance — in stark contrast to his present loneliness and sense of being out of place in the rapidly evolving world. But in thinking of these early events he also began to wonder how time had elusively passed him by. Jakob couldn't help but ask himself where the past seventy years had gone. It truly seemed as if seven decades had come and gone in the blink of an eye. While these early memories were heartwarming, they also weighed heavily on Jakob's heart. He desperately desired something he'd been missing from long ago.

By the winter of 1925 one of Jakob's great nephews, Lewis Mumford, had begun to establish himself as a literary critic. Mumford, who had already authored a couple of books by this time, described himself as a "professor of things in general." One remark his nephew had recently made resonated with Jakob that early morning. "In many lives it is the beginnings that are most significant: the first steps, though seemingly effaced, leave their imprint on everything else that follows."

Mumford could have been writing with his own uncle in mind, but his point might well be expanded to all who attempt to capture their personal history. In fact, psychologists today, in both clinical and non-clinical fields, are actively building a body of evidence to support the idea that how people remember their childhood affects how they think and act in their adult life. As Emory University psychology professor Robyn Fivush pointedly explains, "Our personal memories define who we are."

Like every individual, Jakob learned by experience throughout his life. These life experiences were not only character building, but all of these events combined had also come to shape his personality and outlook. In thinking about his nephew's remarks, Jakob could identify two special moments deeply embedded from his early childhood.

As if reliving his favorite memory, Jakob began typing up the first event, painting a picture with words from a spring morning during his early youth.

> I remember one Easter Sunday when the sonorous sounds of the monster bells of the Cathedral were pealing and seemed to transmit their powerful vibrations through the air to my very frame. My mother listened with me to these majestic sounds, while I followed her with my sisters into the courtyard. We found the nests with the many colored and marbleized Easter eggs. The rabbit had brought these just as he brings them on Easter today.

Some would call Jakob's sense of Easter magic, "innocence." Though he became a critical thinker as he grew up, and tinkered more than most with cause and effect, Jakob maintained a certain openness for magic in his life. And although he acknowledged making various mistakes over the years, his attraction to life's magic was indeed a type of innocence that persisted, from that Easter morning nearly seventy years ago throughout his whole life.

There was a second event that Jakob spontaneously thought of as well. It too had come to define and characterize who Jakob had become. He documented it this way:

> My memory had preserved a print for me. I'm sitting against the wall of [my] home...on a high stool. A small lithograph press is being turned and fed with letter sheets by my father and one of his clerks. I was given

the blank sheets to hold on my knees and had been perched on the high stool to keep me out of mischief, meddling with the ink of the press or with its gears.

Childish curiosity got the best of young Jakob as he recalled leaping into action. "I had climbed up the stairs in the back-building and landed in sight of the press," his narrative read. This lithograph machine was an essential part of his father's work; it was used for printing weekly market reports for his father's customers. Just as little Jakob was about to explore the machine, the elder Schleicher intervened. "I was well enough pleased, but my father had caught me," he typed.

From an early age, Jakob became fascinated with the way machinery operated. Looking back, Jakob realized that his inquisitive and curious nature had also followed him throughout his life, beginning with this one incident. In recalling the story of the machine press, Jakob not only remembered his father's response, but also noted, "I remember [my father] marooned me making me count to ten, then by tens to hundreds, then by hundreds to thousands, then by thousands to hundred thousands, millions and billions.

This occupied me for many mornings, widening my knowledge and my ideas as to quantities and numbers." Even before the start of his formal schooling an emphasis was placed on education. Not only was education used to teach moral and life lessons, as in the case of the machine press, education was occasionally used as a form of discipline. Although unpleasant at the time, looking back, Jakob acknowledged this form of child rearing had come to shape the way he would see the world and the way he approached life. He believed it aided in deepening his character.

JAKOB'S STORY AND THE AMERICAN DREAM

Jakob's father, Adolf, himself a noble example of a hard-working individual, once gave all of his children a task that stood out from the rest. The typewriter keys began clicking a bit faster as Jakob's train of thought headed into a straightaway.

> Our father had put to us the task of memorizing to perfection [Friedrich] Schiller's "Song of the Bell" in its entirety of 10-12 pages of verses. Memorizing came easy to us in those days. The beauties of the Schiller poetry and verse sunk into our young poetic minds readily and filled us with enthusiasm.

Comprised of some 430 lines, "Song of the Bell" is one of the most famous (and longest) German poems in history. Friedrich Schiller crafted this poem after spending a few months in a bell foundry, observing the processes involved in creating a bell. While the poem tells of the technical description of a bell being cast, in a clever way, the author uses the bell casting as an analogy of human existence, complete with life's many possibilities and risks. One theme of this poem reminds us that no one who carries out any work should do it thoughtlessly, but must put all of his heart into everything he does. In having his children memorize this poem, Adolf indirectly instilled his personal beliefs and values, making this a teachable moment in his children's lives.

After the children mastered the poem, Adolf rewarded them by taking his family on an outing—camping at the beach. In vivid detail, Jakob remembered his reward with excitement.

> We had been full of expectancy. We had never looked upon the ocean before. The trip to [Blankenberghe] shore was the crowning reward for our effort. The test of a faultless, smooth recitation from A to Z was gone through by us two elder brothers and some days there-

after, we were climbing towards evening with our father and a friend the long steps that take you from the low street-level of the small town of Blankenberghe, some forty feet high to the top of the dam that flanks the Ocean. The sight of the sea illumined by the setting sun came on us suddenly and left us speechless for the moment; of such a vast expanse we had had no conception or idea; it was a new experience in our young lives. We stayed a couple of days on the shore, enjoying the sight of the sea, sun and strand; we took our combats with the waves as graduate swimmers of the "Bassin de Natation" (swimming pool) of the city of Antwerp and we gathered no end of algae, sea stars, sea urchins and shells.

Having proudly completed the initial phase of his memoir, a few thoughts came to mind. First, these early impressions from his past held more value than he had originally placed on them. Jakob acknowledged that these early events of his life had indeed formed the foundation of who he had become.

Next, as meaningful as these past events were, they were somewhat difficult to look back on. For although these early memories had temporarily taken him out of his isolation, Jakob now longed even more for the security, the happiness and the youthfulness that childhood brings. These memories also brought another desire to the surface—a return for something he had not experienced in a long while. It was as though the happy memories, bearing the weight of the gap he felt inside, wearied under the strain. These memories did, however, give Jakob momentum to continue on with his memoir. Thinking further about his youth and his days of growing up in Europe,

JAKOB'S STORY AND THE AMERICAN DREAM

the lessons and those people who helped shape his beliefs and view of the world came to mind. He was ready to begin the next step of his memoir.

CHAPTER 3

A European Boyhood

Childhood is a short season.
— Helen Hayes, actress and philanthropist

It was a little after 5:00 AM when Jakob removed the latest sheet from the typewriter and placed it face down on the stack containing the first few pages of his memoir. All of these pages were then neatly placed off to the side of his desk and out of the way from the area where he was working. As he had grown accustomed to doing, Jakob briefly paused and thought about the steps needed for taking on his next task. Leaning back in his chair, he carefully and methodically reviewed his notes before starting the next phase of his memoir.

All would agree that children are impressionable and learn by example. Much like new, unmolded clay, children are pliable, but soon become exposed to and are shaped by a wide range of people and experiences. Their cognitive content normally includes their education at home and at school, as well as interacting with their peers, siblings, parents and relatives. Jakob's youth was full of animated and charming stories, many of which contained people or lessons that, even though it was many years later, had still left memorable impressions on him. Highlighting a few of these stories as anecdotes, Jakob was ready to resume working on his memoir.

Aligning another sheet of paper in the typewriter, Jakob began typing, "Our language at home was strictly German." This opening sentence, though simple, spoke volumes. It conveyed the fact that while growing up in a condensed geographic area such as Europe, a wide-array of languages were spoken in his community and throughout the region. In fact, many languages were even taught and encouraged in his home. "From our maid-servants in the nursery we had learned Flemish and Dutch...later [becoming] efficient and correct Dutch scholars," Jakob explained. Managing to briefly recall his first exposure to the French language he continued, "Before entering school at the age of six, I had been coached in French by Mademoiselle Ormond, my (older) sister's teacher."

In all, Jakob became fluent in seven different languages. He considered German, French, and Flemish to be his native tongues, but was also proficient in English, Dutch, Spanish and Portuguese. His classical training also included Latin and Greek, which in the 1860s was considered a standard part of education. But the one household rule remained: German was the only language that was permitted to be formally spoken in the Schleicher home.

There was another point to be considered in this opening sentence as well. While the emphasis was somewhat lost, it was also meant to convey his parent's preservation of their native tongue and their long-held German family heritage. For although Jakob and his siblings were raised in Belgium's historic city of Antwerp, his parents made it a point to pass down to each of their children not only their native tongue, but also their family history and ties to Germany. Jakob could easily recall the numerous occasions throughout his youth when his parents used to recite their family history to him and his siblings.

Originally from Aachen, a city located in Western Germany, Jakob's branch of the Schleicher family traveled east to the German city of Stolberg in the early 1600s where they remained for the next 250 years. When a series of political upheavals began sweeping across Europe in the spring of 1848, an undercurrent of unrest in Germany quickly turned into a revolution. In June of that same year, less than a month after the German government convened to secure a new constitution, his parents, Adolf Schleicher and Emma Langen married in Cologne. But the rioting and insecurity were still fresh in these newlyweds' memory. Adolf and his wife fled Germany to start a family in neighboring Belgium, where they settled in the northern city of Antwerp.

During the late 1840s, however, Belgium was also experiencing its own economic and political difficulties. Although Belgium was safer and more stable than Germany, unemployment and hunger were nonetheless widespread and problematic. Adolph and Emma calculated the risks and attractions Antwerp offered, and ultimately planted roots and began their family there. Located only one hundred miles west of Stolberg, the ancient city of Antwerp bore a strong resemblance to a Dutch or German city. Thus, the German couple had both independence and security while at the same time still having a sense of being "home."

After the birth of his two older sisters, Karl August Jakob Schleicher was born on November 21, 1851. He was named after both of his grandfathers, August Schleicher and Jakob Langen. Reminded throughout his youth that he was not only carrying on the Schleicher surname, but, as he was taught, it came with a responsibility for in his family there was a longstanding family tradition of keeping the surname honorable and respected. Hard work was not only a reflection on him personally; his success or failure was also a reflection on the family's namesake.

Sitting in his library that quiet morning, Jakob came to realize that, from being taught and ultimately mastering numerous languages, learning about his German heritage, and even being named after both of his grandfathers, expectations for him to excel began at an early age. Jakob now reasoned that the knowledge that had been passed down to him had not only helped make him a more, well-rounded individual, but these were in fact foundational pillars that helped build his character and skill set.

Although there were a few other important people and lessons from his European boyhood that he felt also needed mentioning, for now he was content with having typed for a couple of hours. Rising slowly out of his chair and removing his spectacles, Jakob stretched. With the radiola continuing to play in the background, he exited his library to take a short break.

Returning to his library a short time later, Jakob resumed his memoir by typing: "My two older sisters in general set [for] me a good example." From his older siblings he quickly jumped to the two most influential people in his life, his parents. He continued:

> My father supervised my earliest school activities regardless of his own comforts, and would rise in mid-

winter with me at 5:00 AM. After spelling, reading and the rudimentaries of grammar in French and German had been conquered, he assisted me in memorizing no end of recitations, mostly [Jean de] La Fontaine's fables and such pieces [by] Frederic the Great and the Miller of Sans-souci.

While there were countless other examples Jakob could have chosen from, this one illustration fit perfectly how the elder Schleicher engaged his son: not just promoting, but actually participating in Jakob's education.

Jakob's mother had a much different approach and effect. Recounting an episode that summarized his mother's affection toward her children, Jakob chose the following account. Peering back into his past, he recorded a rather frightening event that occurred when he was seven years old.

[Our] house became a hospital. We children were all taken with the deadly epidemic, scarlet fever. This kept my mother active for some six weeks or longer.

This event scared the entire family, no one more so than his mother, Emma. As his mother tended to each of her children, this left an irrevocable impression with Jakob. This memory was in line with his mother's trait of helping others in general. Over the years Jakob's fondness for his mother actually expanded to include every mother, as he added, "We all owe our mothers affection and obedience to the last day of their lives."

There was one other individual Jakob included in his list of those he felt had influenced him the most—a teacher from his days at Athene Royal Elementary School, Monsieur Debognie.

Monsieur Debognie of the 4th grade was most thorough and excelled by the special attention he bestowed individually on each of his 12-15 pupils. He always kept remarkably serious and indulged in jocose and ironical remarks with a most sober face, but woe to the one who then dared to laugh; he would the next moment stand before him, bending his ear and fire some question at the culprit, whom he knew would miss the answer. He would retire, then victoriously having inflicted the punishment for what he considered a breach of discipline.

From his siblings, to his parents, to even a favorite teacher, Jakob found the resourcefulness within himself to give proper credit, even to the smallest degree, to those he felt had the most positive influence on him. But while thinking of these individuals, Jakob also recounted one episode of a less than stellar role model. He began to document his next story, a kind of confession, this way:

> I remember still one of my earliest instructions on Flemish language and ethics at the hand of one of our good-natured nurses. It was in the public park and I had emptied a small beer bottle she had given me to drink, I being probably five years old. Children have been taken with the light Sweetish beer in Belgium since Caesar's time and there is no prejudice against it. After I finished it, she told me to take the bottle by the neck and smash it against the bench on which we were sitting. I did my best, but the bottle was stronger than I and finally she did it for me. This course of education, volunteered by the Flemish maid to form my character, hardly had the sanction of my parents.

His parents would have objected to their son's poor manners in not properly disposing of the bottle and the possibility that his actions could harm other children who came to play in the park.

As these various people and events came to mind, Jakob began to make sense of his past. These events, while completely unconnected, did have something in common. Every person he reflected upon and every episode had indeed left an imprint of the values he came to espouse.

Enriching his thinking skills and his virtue, Jakob briefly reflected on two final subjects from his youth: his exposure to art and religion.

To help cultivate their children's imagination and creativity levels, Jakob's parents made it a point of exposing them to art. "On Sundays we spent hours in contemplation and study of...the Flemish masters, Rubens, Van Dyke, Rembrandt, Quentin Massys, and numerous minor geniuses," Jakob noted. These experiences brought a level of freshness and sentimentality, at the same time creating his unique perspective and view of the world. "The inspiration [we] received filled our minds with ambition and noble ideas, and sustained our daily efforts for work and study and the serious endeavors of life," he concluded.

His parents also laid a foundation of raising all of their children in the Reformed Protestant, or Calvinist, tradition. Jakob attended church regularly, but noted he "did not despise as a Protestant listening to the eloquent Flemish sermon of a Catholic brother or abbe." His days of attending the Athene Royal private school further enhanced his faith as it included daily activities such as prayer, religious courses, and singing in the church choir. "Teacher Herr Holthausen commandeered his classes often to sing in church with great effect," Jakob keenly recounted of his choir teacher.

On the subject of faith, Jakob remembered one item that hung in his Antwerp home during his youth. Sitting in his library that morning all these years later, Jakob could still envision the old mural with clarity. "[On] the broad granite mantel back of the iron stove [was] the large picture of the Madonna and the Christ-child in bright warm colors." Just as this drawing was embedded into the wall of his former home, it had also set into and became part of Jakob's psyche. He explained simply, "It left an impression on me." The mural's content was a tangible sign of a belief deeply rooted in Jakob's Protestant faith. "There is happiness in this and a moral investment of good and sure returns according to the promise attached to the Fourth Commandment of our Catechism. This investment has stood the test of the age of humanity and you need not pay any commissions on it," Jakob explained.

As he started to complete his thoughts on this portion of his life, he began to think back to his teenaged years and how he naturally began wanting his independence. It was around this period of his life that he was permitted to go on educational summer outings. Taking a vacation, for children at least, was not widely practiced, even though school was out of session during the summer months. "We had been convinced by our elders long ago that vacations had been established originally for the needed recreation of teachers and professors, that pupils being still young and pliable and a good deal [of time] at play did not need any vacations, but which should be used faithfully for the rehearsing of what they had learned so far, in order not to forget it. Still, we also had our relaxations and pleasures," Jakob wrote.

Jakob very briefly recounted two outings he went on as a teen. Both outings were memorable, for different reasons. Referencing back to his religious education, Jakob recalled once visiting a Trappist convent where "silence was imposed on all those who are not temporarily in contact with the outer world by their mission and after you enter the convent no voice is heard." While he didn't quite grasp the monastic life, Jakob clearly recalled one detail from his visit to the convent.

> Their most friendly cemetery, bathed in the sun, lay on the South flank of the church building covered with grapevines; there were long rows of simple black wooden cross headings and where the last row ended there was an open grave ready to receive the next brother who would be called away from his silent life to eternity.

Upon leaving this particular excursion Jakob noted thankfully, "It was late in the afternoon when we took our leave and passing through the little gate cut into the big portal we breathed a deep sigh on passing into the outer world, feeling as if we were emerging from the mediaeval age."

His second excursion would be a bit more adventurous and memorable as it would come to teach him a lifelong lesson about independence, liberty and the Fatherland.

CHAPTER 4

Liberty Enlightening the World

Life without liberty is like a body without spirit.
—Kahlil Gibran, poet and philosopher

The following morning Jakob awoke at his customary time of 4:30 AM. His regular morning routine of catching up on current events by reading the morning newspaper while drinking his coffee would have to wait. Jakob had something more pressing to attend to.

Just before 5:00 AM, with a freshly brewed cup of coffee in hand, Jakob made his way into his library. He wanted to continue working on his memoir. His memories from yesteryear had come alive so much that they now captivated him. Rather than the difficult and complicated chore he thought it might be when beginning, he had actually begun to enjoy penning his memoir. Now ready to craft his next story, he powered on his radiola and took a couple of sips of coffee.

In several ways 1865 was a pivotal year. In Jakob's home country of Belgium a new king was crowned for the first time in thirty-four years. Leopold I, a one-time German prince whose reign in Belgium had begun in 1831, died at the age of seventy-four. Upon his death, he was succeeded by his son, Leopold II.

In America, much was at stake as the Civil War entered its fourth year. As the casualty count continued to climb, liberty, like a coin tossed and suspended in mid-air, seemed to hang in the balance. Were the slaves of the South going to be liberated? Was America going to stay permanently divided? By April of 1865 these questions were finally answered. Then Abraham Lincoln, who in the words of United States Minister to Prussia, Norman B. Judd, "had come to symbolize the Republic in all its attributes of the liberty and equality of all men," was assassinated. The leader who had carefully guided the nation during its most fragile period was abruptly taken, causing a power vacuum — yet another crisis in the United States.

The summer of 1865 was also a profound time of learning for young Jakob Schleicher. As a soon-to-be fourteen-year-old, he traveled with his family that summer from their home in Antwerp to the battlefield of Waterloo. As Jakob toured the battleground, not only did he traverse in the footsteps of one of Europe's most influential wars, but it was during this excursion that he came to discover both the true meaning of independence and liberty, as well as gaining a lifelong admiration of his Fatherland, Prussia (Germany).

Coinciding with Jakob's visit to Waterloo, some 250 miles further south in a city called Glavigny near Paris, a meeting was

JAKOB'S STORY AND THE AMERICAN DREAM

taking place. There the seed of liberty was about to be sown. Much like a tree being planted, watered and nurtured—and only after years of attention giving shade—the impact of this meeting would be felt from France across the Atlantic to America. Eventually even Belgium-born Jakob Schleicher came to feel the effects of this historic meeting.

The aftermath of Abraham Lincoln's death was felt both in America and abroad. The division and bitterness between North and South only intensified. In Congress, radical Republicans used Lincoln's death as motivation to push their bills, exacting a heavy price on the South for the "war of rebellion." Further exacerbating an already emotionally raw and splintered country, integration of former slaves and reconstruction proceeded at a much slower pace than originally planned. President Andrew Johnson, Lincoln's vice president and a Southerner, was a weak successor, unable to execute the new laws and steadily losing supporters. As politicians fought over reconstruction and how to move the country forward, tributes to President Lincoln poured in from around the world. From Camden, New Jersey, poet Walt Whitman published his poem "O Captain! My Captain!"

In Europe, Britons and others mourned Lincoln's death as if he had been their own leader. The people of France felt a close-knit bond with America dating back to 1776 and the American Revolution; their sorrow was sincere. As a manifestation of the bond the two countries shared, a national movement began for a gold medal to be cast and given to Mary Todd Lincoln as a tribute to her late husband. The medal was to feature President Lincoln's portrait on one side and an inscription on the reverse: "Lincoln, honest man, abolished slavery, restored the Union, and saved the Republic, without veiling the statue of liberty."

This short statement not only summarized Abraham Lincoln's presidency, but it also briefly described the feelings that the people of France held toward the slain President. The concluding phrase "without veiling the statue of liberty" was meant to honor Abraham Lincoln's ability to preserve both the Union and liberty, despite four years of bitter conflict.

In addition to the longstanding bond these countries shared, the French held America's form of democracy in high regard. Unlike the United States, France did not have the liberties America had in the 1860's. In fact, in this period known as the Second Empire (1852-1870) France's leader, Napoleon III ruled with tyranny.

It was Napoleon's desire to return France to greatness—by his definition, like the days some fifty years prior when his uncle, Napoleon Bonaparte, ruled. Although Napoleon III brought about the rebuilding of Paris and some measurable amount of economic progress, overall it was a frustrating time for the people of France. In an effort to control dissent and reduce the power of his opposition, France's leader implemented strict authoritarian measures, censoring the press and all forms of political expression.

With political gatherings being illegal, one common method of exchanging political ideas was for politicians to arrange "social" dinner parties at their residences. One evening in the summer of 1865, the leader of France's Liberal Party, Eduardo Laboulaye, hosted a small number of literary men, artists and fellow politicians. The evening left an indelible impression on one guest in attendance, a French artist by the name of Frederic-Auguste Bartholdi. Many years later Bartholdi recalled how the conversation that evening "interested me so deeply that it remained fixed in my memory." Mr. Laboulaye and his guests were smoking in the conservatory of his charming retreat

[when] the talk fell upon international relations." Specifically, the conversation focused on the partnership between France and her ally, the United States.

After one guest at the gathering cynically remarked that Americans had no memory of the aid France had provided in 1776 during their War of Independence, without hesitation the host, Laboulaye, passionately exclaimed, "Not so! America's feeling toward France is not one of simple gratitude. It is based on the remembrance of a community of thought and struggles and aspirations. When two hearts have beaten together, something always remains, among nations as among individuals!" Laboulaye, a professor and expert in American history, went on to warmly describe the kinship between both countries as that of "two sisters."

Perhaps one of the most meaningful excursions Jakob Schleicher ever took was when he and his family visited the battlefield at Waterloo. For a young, impressionable teenager, this field trip made the war seem real. Having advanced in his classical education, Jakob's thinking skills were deepening and he was developing logic and reason. For the first time he began to think critically about how one's worldview affects how one draws conclusions. He began creating his very own hypotheses. During this tour Jakob learned a valuable lesson on independence in a way he probably could not have learned elsewhere. He was coming into his own as an independent learner and thinker.

The Battle of Waterloo was a three-day engagement that took place in June, 1815. On many levels it was a defining moment in European history. Although it lasted only a few short days, this conflict reshaped the war-torn continent for a half-century, bringing peace and stability.

Located approximately eight miles south of Brussels in Belgium is the small village of Belle Alliance. Neighboring the larger city of Waterloo, Belle Alliance was the location that both the Battle of Waterloo and Jakob's tour began. "The railroad train took us from Antwerp to Brussels and from there a stage carried us to Belle Alliance, a village located on the main road that traverses the battlefield," Jakob recalled.

As the Schleichers' outing began, their guide provided a prelude describing the lead-up to the Battle of Waterloo. Napoleon Bonaparte had escaped from exile in February 1815 and returned to power in France for a period known as the "Hundred Days" (111 actual days). After Europe's ruling authority, the Congress of Vienna, declared Napoleon an outlaw, an alliance of seven countries (The Seventh Coalition) was mobilized to defeat him. The seven countries included Great Britain, Russia, Prussia, Sweden, Austria, the Netherlands, and a number of German states. In an effort to stay in power, Napoleon tried to dissuade the Seventh Coalition from invading France. Once this attempt failed, Napoleon gave the order for France's army to cross north into the United Kingdom of the Netherlands (present-day Belgium) and attack before coalition troops could mobilize.

Not long into the tour, a short overview of battle tactics of this campaign was given. An extended artillery bombardment began the initial phase. This was followed by an infantry and cavalry attack. Jakob seemed to have made a mental note about the accuracy and intensity of these artillery bombings as two particular details caught his attention. "To begin with...there was the tavern of Belle Alliance...showing some cannon balls imbedded in its walls," Jakob distinctly recalled. Also, "a couple of miles on the same road further toward the center of the fight stood the monument erected in honor of the English Lieutenant Colonel, Sir [Alexander] Gordon, who fell at that spot."

Gordon, whose monument is probably one of the best known, lost his leg during the battle from a cannon ball attack. (Gordon succumbed to his injury the following morning.) These harrowing artillery bombardments caused massive carnage by decapitating and disemboweling men and horses.

The tour guide explained to Jakob's group that, for those infantry soldiers who were fortunate enough to outmaneuver artillery rounds, dodging musket fire became their next obstacle to traverse. Lethal from several hundred feet away, especially when fired en masse, the low-speed iron balls were easy to spot and track as they approached in their parabolic flight path. Soldiers of that era were considered cowards if they ducked from oncoming rounds; thousands thus died from musket fire.

Battle tactics of the early 1800s commonly dictated that as opposing armies continued to fight, the distance between them gradually became closer. When the gap between the two armies closed to fifty paces or so, they charged each other with bayonets drawn. When the charging cavalries met, soldiers by the dozens were run through and trampled over. Those who remained standing fought valiantly to the death, often becoming dismembered or maimed in the process.

One British soldier who fought in the Battle of Waterloo wrote home, giving his father the following account:

> The French cavalry charged the British line of infantry three different times, and did much execution, until we were obliged to form squares of battalions, in order to turn them, which was executed in a most gallant manner, and many hundreds of them never returned. Still they sent up fresh forces and, as often, we beat them back.

The first forty-eight hours of this battle saw numerous clashes and exchanges around Waterloo. The Schleichers' tour also visited these same locations. "[Taking] in the many distant points over which the various armies marched and the locations for whose capture the battle raged forth and back, kept us trampling all day long from one village to another and from one monument to another," Jakob wrote. "The lunch hour found us on top of the big hill several hundred feet high. In the shade of the giant stone lion—the national monument of the Dutch—the entire battlefield could be surveyed," Jakob vividly remembered.

On the third day of fighting, the final battle took place. Napoleon delayed the start of the battle until almost midday, to allow the ground to dry from the previous night's rains. Ideally, waiting for the ground to dry would have allowed the French artillery and cavalry to better maneuver and tire less quickly, but Napoleon's decision to postpone fighting cost him dearly.

At 11:30 AM the French opened fire on a pivotal strategic position: Hougoumont Farm. It was defended by the Duke of Wellington and his British forces. During the tour, Jakob recounted, "We found the ruins of the old farm Hougoumont, a quite large and extensive establishment surrounded by a seven-foot-high brick wall into which breaches for guns and cannons had been broken for its defense. It had been turned into a stronghold by the French and was abandoned and recaptured several times during the three-day combat."

Wellington and Napoleon both believed that Hougoumont was the key to the Battle of Waterloo. As a result, both men sent large resources to the area throughout the final day of fighting. Wellington assigned twenty-one battalions—equivalent to 12,000 troops—to the area, later explaining, "The success of the battle of Waterloo depended on the closing of the gates of Hougoumont." For his part, Napoleon sent thirty-three battalions or 14,000 troops to the same area. The battle for Hougoumont raged throughout the day with no clear or decisive winner. In what would become a defining moment in his life, Jakob proudly discovered not only how this battle concluded, but also how cause and effect was not limited to the sciences, physics or engineering.

Napoleon's decision to delay battle had allowed some 80,000 coalition reinforcements to arrive late that afternoon. "[Gebhard Leberecht von] Blücher and his Prussians came to the rescue of the despairing Englishmen under Wellington and turned the tide of the battle against the French army," Jakob learned during the tour. "The law of retribution, of which our modernists fail to find traces in history seemed to us to need no monument on this battlefield as we were trailing the struggle over this vast expanse now covered with crops of grains of all kinds and filled us with awe and solemnity."

Von Blücher's rescuing of the Seventh Coalition had triggered in Jakob a sense of admiration and pride. From an early age, Jakob had been taught about his German heritage and took pride in his lineage. On this day however, his view transcended to include his Fatherland being a force for good in the world. "After a long period of oppression and humiliation, more so for Germany than the other similarly affected nations, the day for joint resistance had finally come and 'blood and iron' had brought deliverance through temporary union," Jakob noted.

Accounting for nearly one fourth of all soldiers involved the Battle of Waterloo, by day's end 40,000 to 50,000 soldiers had perished. For Blücher and Prussia some 7,000 men died. Wellington had lost 15,000 soldiers in this one skirmish alone. That evening, after the battle ended, Wellington refused to leave the battlefield. Usually an unemotional man, he continued to ride his horse to and fro, surveying the carnage, even after being told his life was at risk. Weeping, Wellington simply replied: "The battle's won. My life's of no consequence now."

For Napoleon Bonaparte's French army, 25,000 men had perished, with another 8,000 taken prisoner. To France's emperor, this loss of life meant nothing. His own life and reputation remained all-important. The dead were simply "numbers" — a byproduct of war. Napoleon's proclamation from 1802 had finally come to pass. "My power proceeds from my reputation, and my reputation from the victories I have won. My power would fall if I were not to support it with more glory and more victories. Conquest has made me what I am; only conquest can maintain me." Napoleon Bonaparte's power and conquest was now gone. His reign over France, and his dream of ruling the world, had finally come to an end.

Jakob absorbed much that day and heading back home, remembered: "It was dark and quite late when we reached the stage at Belle Alliance for return to Brussels and Antwerp." After an entire day on the former battlefield, it was a sobering journey back to Antwerp. While it was exciting to hear about the various engagements as the tour guide described them, the enormous number of casualties seemed overwhelming and difficult to grasp. In trying to process all he had seen, heard and read, Jakob was conflicted. Besides learning about the actual battle, Jakob was bothered by the oppression Napoleon Bonaparte had imposed on France. Of Napoleon's tyranny and absolutism, his callousness and seemingly self-serving motives, Jakob observed, "We have seen how selfishness will make the leaders of nations blind and separate their people when they should stand united." For the people of France, where was liberty? After all, "Liberty, Equality, Fraternity" was a slogan the French adopted in 1789 during the French Revolution.

It was only after the overthrow of the monarchy that Napoleon Bonaparte began to suppress political and civil liberties, stating, "What the French people want is equality, not liberty."

He had cleverly used equality as a means to bring himself unprecedented power, admiration and loyalty. In doing so he effectively repressed and subverted liberty. Although many of the less fortunate believed Napoleon was an advocate for the poor, in truth he believed that liberty was a form of anarchy. Liberty threatened the efficiency of the state, and had to be suppressed at all costs in order to protect the leader's power and authority.

Jakob wondered why the people of France sacrificed their liberty and fraternity. What were their motives? What chain of reasoning led them to recklessly follow their dictator? "Had we not been imbued with the history and the literature that belonged to the period of the vainglorious despot and a nation ever ready to be misled through its vanity and thirst for glory?" Jakob wondered. By 1865, some fifty years after the Battle of Waterloo had taken place, tyranny and authoritarianism were once again in force under Napoleon III. But liberty was about to be cultivated in France again.

As the dinner and social in Glavigny continued that summer evening, the host and his guests were discussing the recently concluded Civil War in America. For Eduardo Laboulaye, America's ability to overcome the divisive issue of slavery was especially meaningful, as he was a close observer and supporter of America. Even among the French, there was a sense of victory and admiration that America had overcome oppression and ended slavery. For the first time in America's history, freedom and liberty now existed for all its citizens.

As the conversation continued that evening, Mr. Laboulaye offered a surprising suggestion to his guests: "Wouldn't it be wonderful if people in France gave the United States a great monument as a lasting memorial to independence and thereby showed that the French government was also dedicated to the idea of human liberty? If a monument were to be built in America as a memorial of independence, it would be most natural to have it built by a united effort, to make it the common work of both nations." These were not lofty words simply to make the host sound good in front of his guests, nor was the idea of gifting a monument to America simply a noble or kind gesture. As a well-recognized scholar, jurist and abolitionist, and as France's leading expert on the United States, Eduardo Laboulaye's words were sincere and held weight. For starters, he was keenly aware that the form of government in the United States was an inspiration for other aspiring republics. It was also Eduardo Laboulaye's strongly held belief that America was the repository of liberty in a world where most nations, including France, were still ruled by undemocratic governments. These convictions also explain Eduardo Laboulaye's active role in French politics as he sought to depose Napoleon III in hopes of establishing a lasting democratic form of government in France. With the recent Union victory and abolishment of slavery, this "memorial of independence" became the ideal gift to honor the United States. It was Mr. Laboulaye's hope that a monument would in turn inspire his fellow French reformers to restore republican liberties being suppressed under the rule of Napoleon III.

That evening all of Laboulaye's guests agreed that a "Monument of Independence" should be gifted to the United States in 1876 (to mark the centennial of the American Revolution). But Eduardo Laboulaye and Frederic Bartholdi's vision would not take shape immediately. In fact, Lady Liberty would not be presented to America until 1886, some twenty-one years after its proposal at the house party in France.

JAKOB'S STORY AND THE AMERICAN DREAM

Originally created to celebrate a common democratic experience that France and the United States had once shared, the Statue of Liberty was also designed to commemorate the end of the Civil War, thus becoming the symbol of a new hope for the exemplary democracy America displayed to the world. While it's true that liberty existed for some in America prior to 1865, France's monument "Liberty Enlightening the World," had a human face and was a tangible object for all to see. Laboulaye once fittingly described liberty as, "the mother of a family that watches over the cradle of her children, that protects consciences ... Liberty is the sister of Justice and of Mercy, mother of Equality, Abundance, and Peace." Eduardo Laboulaye and his close associate, Frederic-Auguste Bartholdi, helped bring this idea to the forefront of the American experience. From one historic discussion, an iconic symbol was born.

For Jakob, the visit to Waterloo was more than just a history lesson or a family outing. Rather, it became a turning point during his youth. As a result of the heroics of Field Marshal von Blücher, Jakob's view of Prussia (precursor to modern day Germany) was elevated. Now viewed as a force for good in the world, Jakob held this view of the Fatherland throughout his life. But also as a teenager, Jakob had begun thinking of his own independence. As he critically analyzed this historic battle, later integrating its lessons with reflections on America's Civil War, Jakob realized that independence, whether for a single individual or an entire country, is the freedom from outside control *and* the ability to self-govern. Liberty, on the other hand, is associated with people of an independent country having freedom, rights and the ability to make their own choices. Jakob observed how, at one juncture, the people of France did not have liberty under Napoleon's rule, and how the newly freed slaves of

America were now granted liberty. "Life without liberty is like a body without spirit," poet and philosopher Kahlil Gibran noted. Likewise Jakob and millions of others around the world found America's spirit of liberty worth emulating. Jakob had no idea in 1865, but a decade later he would be given the opportunity to travel to the United States and experience first-hand his own independence and the liberties America provided.

In documenting this important episode from his past, Jakob failed to realize that it had taken up a good portion of his morning. Now at 9:00 AM, it was time to step away from his typewriter and relax. Jakob was now ready to read his newspaper and go about the rest of his day.

CHAPTER 5

The Otto-Langen Experiment

*Your name will become famous enough in time;
I shall see to that.*
—Eugen Langen to Nicholas Otto, 1876

Later that afternoon Jakob again returned to his library to work on his memoir. Certain he had touched on all key points relating to his youth he was prepared to move onto the next stage of his life story: his transition into early adulthood. Jakob took this opportunity to describe how, during his adolescent years he became interested in a newly emerging technological advancement, the gas-powered engine. Marking this period of his life his passion for learning about the gas-powered engine not only translated into him dedicating many hours of study to its history, but it also kindled a fire that captivated him for the next three decades. Rather quickly Jakob discovered his calling and decided to pursue a career in this field.

But as he also noted, there was one other significant detail that occurred during this transitional stage of his life. Having already learned the core values of hard work and study, teenaged Jakob Schleicher began to notice and observe admirable qualities from a few of his closest acquaintances. Emulating these same positive character traits, a level of confidence and dexterity soon emerged. As his personality flourished, Jakob also began to set long-term goals for himself. Gradually maturing into an adult, he became a polished and well-rounded individual. Confident that this was the right direction for his memoir to take, he resumed by typing:

> The general history of the gas engine and of its evolution from the first experiments to the present modern motor has kept growing, not only in volume, but also in age.

The history of the gas engine came to include two of the Schleicher brothers: Jakob and his younger brother, Adolph. Jakob and Adolph both became involved in the engineering field thanks to their uncle, Eugen Langen, who was co-owner of the successful manufacturing company that was producing Europe's finest gas-powered engines. Having devoted over two decades to this field as an engineer, Jakob both witnessed, and was part of, numerous advancements in this field. Thus, as a result of his exposure and accomplishments to engineering, it became his area of expertise. This was one of his proudest lifetime achievements, and he cherished his memories from his days as an engineer, always having much to say on this subject.

Jakob found himself wondering: *How could one not appreciate the gains and strides technology has made without acknowledging those in the past who built the foundation of what became such a wide ranging and large industry?* Although there were just a few individuals from the past who helped develop the gas engine, there were many more who helped create the industry it evolved into. As a means to acknowledge those innovators and pioneers from yesteryear, who—without hard work and a vision would never have afforded him or his brother the opportunity to enter this field to begin with—and with a sense of gratitude, Jakob spent a little bit of time describing the history of the gas engine.

Inspired by French engineer Phillipe Lebon's "double-acting" engine of 1801, the first attempt at commercially manufacturing and selling gas engines began in 1860 when Belgian engineer Étienne Lenoir patented an internal combustion engine. Shortly after Lenoir began marketing his engine, it was quickly considered by many to be the heir apparent to the steam engine. Lenoir's invention, a "two-stroke" engine, added a carburetor and a liquid hydrocarbon (petrol) to Lebon's original idea. Prior to these early internal combustion engines, all previous engines, like the steam engine, were of the external combustion variety. With precision and detail, Jakob noted that, although Lenoir failed to compress the vapors his engine produced, he did benefit from the newer techniques, better materials and equipment that was unavailable in 1801.

Also around 1860, an eighteen-year-old named Nicholas August Otto was making a meager living as a traveling salesman selling coffee, teas and sugar along Germany's western border. Lenoir's new engine caught Nicholas Otto's imagination and provided Otto many hours of learning as he studied its unique two-step process. In addition to the type of fuel it used, Otto discovered what made Lenoir's engine unique: it operated without any internal compression. Although a total of five hundred of Lenoir's engines were sold worldwide, the popularity of this particular engine model faded rather quickly. In charging $400 for a ½-horsepower engine and $600 for a 1-horsepower engine, Lenior's engine never became practical or affordable enough to catch on. Nonetheless, Étienne Lenoir's early engine was still considered a technological breakthrough, and Lenoir's presence as an early pioneer of the gas engine remained strong for a number of years.

Nicholas Otto's fascination and curiosity with the Lenoir engine continued. With no formal education, and by having taught himself the basic principles of engine operation, Nicholas Otto's ongoing experimenting, revisions and improvements of this product began to pay dividends. By 1861 Otto had started developing a working prototype gas engine. Believing he had created a marketable product, Otto spent large amounts of money patenting his engine concept throughout Europe during the early 1860s. But after a year of patenting and marketing this engine, Nicholas Otto rapidly began facing a money shortage. This German salesman could neither establish a niche to profit from his invention, nor proceed any further in promoting this promising engine.

Nicholas Otto and Eugen Langen. Photos courtesy of Deutz AG.

In 1864 Nicholas Otto and Eugen Langen met. With an engineering background, Eugen Langen saw that although imperfect,

JAKOB'S STORY AND THE AMERICAN DREAM

Nicholas Otto's engine had potential. Both men believed they could collectively profit by becoming business partners. Nicholas Otto felt this opportunity might afford him the chance to further experiment and improve his engine, while Eugen Langen saw unlimited opportunities and profits. Allocating the funds necessary to establish a business, Eugen Langen agreed to partner with Nicholas Otto. Together they founded the world's first gas-powered engine factory, naming it N. A. Otto & Company.

For a moment Jakob's attention shifted from the gas engine's history to his Uncle Eugen.

Jakob had developed a fondness toward his uncle, like he would for an older brother. Eugen was eighteen years older than Jakob, and thanks in large part to Eugen's interest in machinery, Jakob's involvement in this field flourished. It was through this common interest that the two bridged their age difference.

From an early age, both Jakob and Eugen were intrigued with the concept of cause and effect and were fascinated with the dynamics of how machinery operated. Referencing back to the episode with his father's lithograph press machine, Jakob seemed to have a predisposition and curiosity as to the workings of machinery. For Eugen, his interest in this field eventually set him on a course to study mechanical engineering, chemistry and chemical technology in technical school. After his schooling was completed, Eugen went to work for his father as an engineer in the family's sugar factory. While Eugen used his education and considerable talents to design a number of pieces of equipment used at the sugar refinery, teenaged Jakob observantly took note. Similar to the role of a teacher, Eugen took the opportunity to explain and illustrate to his young nephew, the pupil, some of the basic concepts he had learned in technical school. Jakob's interest in this field grew as he matured, but there was one other quality Jakob noticed that his uncle possessed. Eugen had an ability to visualize infinite possibilities. Whether it was seeing the potential in Nicholas Otto's fallible engine, or crafting various instruments for the sugar factory, Eugen was a forward-thinker. In witnessing his uncle's ability to conceptualize, Jakob became inspired. Adopting this same attribute, Jakob also tried to expand on his own creativity and become open to an array of possibilities.

Within a few short years of Eugen Langen and Nicholas Otto going into business together, Otto made a number of important improvements to the engine. By 1867 a newer, sleeker atmospheric engine was consuming a fraction of the fuel other engines of the period were using. The basic principle of this refined version was the use of a flywheel to better regulate each working stroke, as well as the use of a flame ignition which replaced battery and spark ignitions from earlier prototypes. Then, the opportunity for Nicholas Otto and Eugen Langen came to challenge their closest competitor, Étienne Lenoir, for engine supremacy. This showdown took place at the 1867 Exhibition in Paris, France.

Jakob was only fifteen years old at the time, but even after all these years he could still recall the story. "In 1867 the Langen and Otto atmospheric engine became the rival of the Lenoir engine," Jakob recounted. "It was noisy, but its gas consumption was but one-fourth of that of the Lenoir motor." At the Paris Exhibition the judges immediately took notice of the Otto engine's low fuel consumption. Puzzled and dismayed, they ordered repeat tests. Lenoir and his team of engineers believed there was trickery taking place, that Otto and Langen were somehow using a hidden gas line. At the end of the competition

JAKOB'S STORY AND THE AMERICAN DREAM

when the tests were confirmed and no hidden lines were detected, the Otto-Langen engine was declared the winner and awarded the gold medal.

With the amount of publicity and recognition their engine received, there would be no need for Otto and Langen to invest a large sum in marketing. "This invention very soon commanded a phenomenal sale," Jakob explained. Following the Paris Exhibition, demand for the fuel-efficient engine quickly spiked. Langen and Otto were unprepared for the onslaught of orders they received. the N.A. Otto & Company had reached their production limits and were unable to produce engines fast enough. Operating out of a cramped workshop that no longer suited their needs, and short of both supplies and finances, the two co-owners were forced to reorganize. As part of their company's expansion, a new, larger facility was purchased in the Cologne suburb of Deutz. They also agreed to sell their patent rights and have their engines produced by an affiliated company outside of Germany. This decision was made in order to meet consumers' growing demands. The first affiliated representatives were the Crossley Brothers of England in 1869.

As he journeyed back to the year 1869, sitting at his typewriter, Jakob's attention was once again diverted from the history of the gas engine. This was the year that his grandfather (Eugen Langen's father) passed away. "A grandfather is someone with silver in his hair and gold in his heart," goes the old adage. This embodiment was the way Jakob remembered his grandfather, and this was a quality that Jakob tried to live by with his own grandchildren as well. Unable to pass up the opportunity, Jakob typed the following passage regarding his beloved grandpa.

The son of a village school teacher and organist, he had prepared himself for the same career in his early youth and while teaching the children of various villages...some businessman in the then small industrial town Solingen engaged him subsequently to tutor his children, but finding him more valuable as assistant in his business made him in time his associate. He became well to do and buying sugar-refinery in Cologne he had moved to that town. To his grandchildren he liked to tell of his experiences as a village teacher, rehearsing to them many an amusing anecdote. At night we often gathered around him at the grand piano and would sing to the touching and solemn chords which he had learned to master during his early years as an organist. He was a member of the City Council of Cologne and had been honored by titles and decorations for activities undertaken in the public interest, Jakob pleasantly recounted.

But Jakob also remembered his grandfather more for being around his joy and pleasure than his achievement and awards. "My grandfather was a venerable gentleman, of medium stature, of serious disposition and of extreme kindness, whose presence would put my cousins and myself always on the best of our behavior."

In August of 1869, just as Jakob was beginning his schooling to become an engineer, his grandfather passed away. His grandfather's large three-acre property was soon sold. Frequented numerous times—not only throughout Jakob's youth, but during all of his grandchildren's early years—it was commonly referred to as "the great paradise."

After his death, the great paradise of his grandchildren was converted into streets and filled with residences and there is nothing left of it but the memory in the minds of a fair number of surviving old men and women at one time young and filling lawns, paths and bowers with their merriment.

Jakob's fondness of his grandfather never faded, nor had the valuable lesson of what it meant to have a golden heart.

As demand for Nicholas Otto's engine continued to steadily increase into the 1870s, business partner Eugen Langen's responsibilities also increased. While Nicholas Otto worked on improving his engine, Eugen Langen was tasked with operating not one, but two businesses. As a result of his father's death, Eugen was now in charge of and oversaw the daily operation of the family's sugar factory, in addition to his responsibilities at the engine manufacturing plant. Carrying on his father's warm and tranquil spirit, Eugen Langen showed genuine concern for his employees. He viewed them as essential resources for his business operations. For several years, both of his commercial enterprises increased their production and profits.

By late 1871 Jakob's younger brother, Adolph, had completed high school. Although deep down he wanted to become a physician, like Jakob, Adolph was inspired by his Uncle Eugen to pursue a career in engineering. Agreeing to do so, Adolph began his schooling for an engineering degree in Cologne in hopes of one day joining the family business.

In early 1872, Eugen Langen and Nicholas Otto's engine business incorporated and was renamed Gasmotorenfabrik Deutz (Deutz Gas Engine Factory). Within eight years of their first meeting, Nicholas Otto and Eugen Langen had established themselves as the leaders in gas-powered engine technology. Eugen Langen's original vision for Nicholas Otto's invention had paid off. He correctly assumed that the gas engine was the technology of the future. Thus far their experiment was a success.

Looking to keep the Deutz company ahead of their competitors, as well as staying on the cutting edge of technology, Eugen Langen sought out the best talent he could find and hired two of the most knowledgeable men in the industry at that time, Gottlieb Daimler and Wilhelm Maybach. Gottlieb Daimler became the company's technical director while Wilhelm Maybach was designated as the chief designer.

Upon being hired at Deutz, Wilhelm Maybach immediately was given the task of redesigning Nicholas Otto's atmospheric engine for the purpose of making it more economical. Realizing his engine had reached its maximum potential, Nicholas Otto along with Gottlieb Daimler and designer Wilhelm Maybach began exploring a newer, more powerful four-cycle engine. But, much like an un-lubricated engine, friction soon began to surface between Otto and Daimler. As work was underway at the Deutz plant for the production of a new engine, Langen took on to two additional new hires: his nephews, Jakob and Adolph Schleicher.

Besides vying for a larger portion of the market, there was growing concern within the Deutz management team over possibly falling behind their competitors, as various forms of engines were reported to be in the manufacturing stages. Hot-air engines, compression engines and atmospheric engines were all rumored to be released in the near future. With America's Centennial Exhibition less than a year away, Deutz management pondered new ways to distinguish themselves from their rivals. The Centennial Exhibition was to be an opportunity for manufacturers from

JAKOB'S STORY AND THE AMERICAN DREAM

around the globe to display their wares and modern gadgetry to a world audience.

Aware of the fact that technology in America was rapidly evolving despite the difficult social reforms of Reconstruction, Eugen Langen believed the time was ideal to introduce a gas-powered engine into the American market. By late 1875 Deutz management decided to send a delegation of engineers to America for the upcoming exhibition. Uncle Eugen selected his nephews to showcase this new product at the exhibition. As Jakob noted in his memoir, following the exhibition, Deutz was planning to establish a subsidiary company much like the Crossley Brothers operation in England to build and sell the Otto engine in America. Noting how he and his younger brother Adolph were asked to relocate to America in order to produce and sell engines for the parent company, Deutz, Jakob pecked out on his typewriter, "Mr. Langen and Dr. Nicholas Otto...selected as their representatives the gentlemen [brothers Jakob and Adolph Schleicher who] became identified with the Otto engine in a permanent manner as its manufacturers in Philadelphia." With their personnel now chosen for this business venture, a series of logistical issues needed solving. More importantly, an exhibit needed to be prepared and finalized.

Jakob closed this portion of his memoir by recounting how, at the start of 1876, a confident Eugen Langen told his long-time business partner and company director, Nicholas Otto, "Your name will become famous enough in time; I shall see to that." With this final passage Jakob retired for the evening.

CHAPTER 6

Jakob's American Dream Begins

*To gild with gold, to paint the lily...
is wasteful and ridiculous excess.*
—William Shakespeare, *King John*, 1595

The following morning was a Tuesday. The cold winter days of 1925 had brought temperatures down into the twenties in Jakob's hometown of Merchantville and across the rest of New Jersey. At 4:30 AM Jakob awoke to a chill in the air along with a sore and scratchy throat. Getting out of bed he noticed that although it was not extremely painful, it was a little difficult for him to swallow. Gradually, Jakob shuffled his way into the bathroom where he felt a strong gust of cold air; someone had left the bathroom window open overnight allowing a draft to circulate throughout the house. Closing the window, he tried the home remedy of gargling with warm salt water. This brought only minimal relief.

Jakob then worked his way to the kitchen where he prepared his morning cup of coffee. As had become his habit lately, Jakob went back upstairs into his library and prepared his work area for writing. He turned on the radiola, placed his coffee on the desk and got out a blank sheet of paper. Only slightly distracted by the sore throat, he was ready to move along into the next stage of his memoir.

The Gilded Age was the dawn of a new chapter in America. It signified the end of postwar Reconstruction and anticipated the Industrial Revolution at the turn of the century.

Mark Twain and Charles Warner, popular authors of the period, found inspiration in Shakespeare's declaration "To gild with gold, to paint the lily...is wasteful and ridiculous excess" for their 1873 novel *The Gilded Age: A Tale of Today*. This satirical work described the cultural excesses the authors observed taking place in America. These excesses came to include corporate and individual corruption, which they attributed to a zeitgeist of altruism and self-denial that had somehow twisted itself into self-indulgence. America was, in their estimation, stuck in an unhealthy habit of living for the moment. The novel showcased various indulgences, its title eventually becoming a shorthand reference point to this era.

For all its faults, the Gilded Age was an era of unprecedented progress. It was marked by numerous changes that included social and political reform, revolutionary inventions in both the industrial and technological fields, as well as the expansion of America's West. It was also during this thirty-year span that eight new states were admitted into the Union and the first Transcontinental Railroad linked America's west coast with its east coast.

It was during this period that America transformed itself, not only growing in size, but also fundamentally changing its agrarian philosophy. Having once valued independent rural farming and simple living, the Gilded Age saw America evolve into an industrial autocracy. But this transition was not simple and seamless. As Mark Twain and Charles Warner observed, a "virus" had begun to invade America. This virus — individualism — was perhaps a reaction against the collective changes of repairing the Civil War's wounds. At any rate, the country was now engrossed in making money. Fortunes were being made, but at what cost? Many Americans' Gilded Age experience was anything but golden.

Industrialism circa 1870 — and its attendant values of progress, profit and wealth — became the new reality. Literature such as Mark Twain's *The Gilded Age* and William Homes McGuffy's *McGuffey Reader* series for schoolchildren continued to promote honesty and piety. These remained influential in society; however, for those who profited the most during this era there existed a double standard.

Often unprepared for the power with which wealth imbued them, some in America's upper class adopted an "all-for-me" mentality. The Puritan code of simple living had begun to lose its influence. Moral purity, respect for God, as well as the traditional practices of education, earning a living, attending church, and family centeredness — arguably, all the values the country was initially founded upon — began disappearing from the American lifestyle.

Americans began moving from the country into growing cities, abandoning farm life for working in factories and offices. The Gilded Age became known as the era of industrialists and "robber barons" with the likes of Carnegie, Rockefeller, J.P. Morgan and Vanderbilt making their fortunes, while the working class paid a heavy price. Other entrepreneurs, industrial go-getters, and even government officials, all concentrated on making a quick buck. With no unions or federal labor laws yet in place, men, women and children all commonly worked in excess of seventy hours a week, frequently in unsafe working conditions. Many of these laborers paid with their health and well-being, and all worked for minimal pay.

As the economy expanded, millions of immigrants from around the world left their native countries, crossing vast oceans to make America their new home. Between 1870 and 1900 nearly twelve million immigrants arrived in the United States, each one with the hope of a new beginning. For most of these new immigrants, however, technical job opportunities were limited as most lacked basic numeracy and logistical skills. The average American's income during this period was only $375 a year. Nevertheless, America was the new world that many from around the globe dreamed of. Indeed, the very fabric of America was transforming into a new and more modern society.

Jakob's inner journey took him back to late 1875, the time just before he came to America. He could recall the date distinctly: December 6. The mere memory of those last weeks before traveling to America piqued Jakob's anxiety.

The *SS Deutschland* was a German passenger steamship that had been in service for nine years. On the evening of December 6 this ship, captained by Eduard Brickenstein, was navigating through blizzard-like conditions on a voyage from Bremerhaven, Germany to New York when it veered off course and ran aground, sinking off England's coast in a region known as Kentish Knock. Although few details about the sinking emerged initially, news soon spread across Europe. Survivors

JAKOB'S STORY AND THE AMERICAN DREAM

later reported that the liner struck the shallow sea floor, resulting in a stress fracture to the ship's propeller. As the ship became incapacitated, it took on large amounts of water. All passengers on board were immediately ordered by the crew to abandon ship. Seventy-eight of the *SS Deutschland's* 213 passengers drowned.

Sitting quietly in front of his typewriter, Jakob then thought back to January 10, 1876. This was the day he boarded a ship bound for America. At twenty-four years of age Jakob Schleicher was about to take the biggest step of his life. As he prepared for the voyage, one could easily envision his parents, Adolf and Emma, waving goodbye to their son and cringing at the fresh memory of the *SS Deutschland*. Although he too was nervous about the trip, Jakob tried to reassure his mother that he would be fine. Still, saying goodbye had a paralyzing effect on his mother for some time afterwards. After all, Emma reasoned, her son was traveling four thousand miles across an ocean—anything could happen. As he sat quietly in his library Jakob was amazed at how vividly he remembered leaving home.

While Jakob's objective for traveling to America had been spelled out, many questions still remained. How would America's industrialists receive the concept of a new gas-powered engine? If America did not embrace this new technology, how long would the experiment last? How would the journey and new situation affect Jakob personally—what would he see? Who would he meet? And what else was in store for him going to this unfamiliar place? This journey would soon become the beginning of Jakob's American Dream.

The term *American Dream* was not yet in use in 1876, but for Jakob and those living outside of America, moving to a new world where prosperity was not dictated by being born into royalty would have been difficult, if not impossible, to conceptualize. Could a place even exist where all citizens, from peasants to a country's leader, have an opportunity to excel and become prosperous? Was there such a place that granted freedom and liberty equally to all of its citizens? For someone to travel to a land where all of these things were possible would, much like a dream, have probably seemed unrealistic.

Many who were living in America in the 1870s and 1880s were already aware of the opportunities and abundance this country had to offer. John W. Britton, president of a New York bank, for example, stated the following in his testimony before the Senate Committee on Education and Labor in 1883: "This is certainly a glorious country for opportunity. A man has no stone upon his head here unless he carries it voluntarily. He has a clear road if he wants to go up."

Jakob Schleicher. Photo courtesy: Chronicle of the Langen Family Assn.

In a similar fashion, an anonymous immigrant who arrived in America in 1850 wrote of America's limitless resources:

"...any man or woman without a family are fools that would not venture and come to this plentiful country where no man or woman ever hungered or ever will and where you will not be seen naked." America, in all her majesty, was indeed a new world for many a newcomer.

Transatlantic travel had improved somewhat by 1876, but even during the best of times, the trip was choppy and unpleasant. At its worst, traveling in the open sea was downright rough and sickening. Steamships cut the average length of time it took to make the 3,700-mile Atlantic crossing from fourteen days to just over seven days. Passage rates ranged from eight dollars for third class, to twenty-five dollars for first class with all passengers being provided three cooked meals per day. Living conditions varied, depending on which deck one occupied.

For the poorest immigrants, who used their life savings for passage to America, conditions were deplorable. They traveled in the steerage deck with animals (and animal waste) and the associated foul odors. They were packed tightly together, and fought over insufficient rations of food and clean water. A ship's surgeon once described this mode of travel by stating, "the torments of hell might in some degree resemble [their] suffering."

For wealthier passengers in first class, transatlantic travel included a well-ventilated cabin, which was almost always shared by four people. Within certain guidelines, alcoholic beverages and smoking were permitted as an added luxury.

Alone in his library Jakob thought about his trip to America. His voyage was in fact nowhere near as unpleasant as for some of the other passengers on board. Jakob shared a cabin with a well-recognized mechanic, inventor and author of the period, John Richards. In 1894, eighteen years after this voyage, Richards published his account of their trip to America in his magazine,

Industry, a monthly magazine devoted to science, engineering and mechanical arts.

"The editor of this journal was a fellow-passenger and roommate with Mr. Schleicher when he first came out to this country. On the journey [I] examined data from the works at Deutz, which was then the most completely-organized establishment of the kind that had come to notice," an impressed Mr. Richards noted.

Undoubtedly, meeting a fellow passenger who was knowledgeable about the engineering field must have brought some solace to Jakob during his voyage. He found another comfort, too: an educational handbook called *The German in America.*

Beginning in 1852 all German immigrants who traveled to America received a copy of this handbook, which was printed bilingually in English and German. It was meant to provide new immigrants important insight into the spirit and nature of America. Although not traveling from Germany per se, Jakob identified himself as German and was of course fluent in the German language, so he received a copy of this handbook during his trip.

Written by a pastor from Massachusetts, F.W. Bogen, *The German in America* begins warmly: "A great blessing meets the German immigrant the moment he steps upon [American] shores." Among its many nuggets of practical advice, the handbook includes this legal information:

> You have the right to remain with your baggage on board the ship forty-eight hours after your arrival. Make use of this privilege. Do not be in a hurry. Take time. Go quietly from your ship along the wharf, and you will see lying there the steamboats which are bound for Philadelphia, Albany and other places.

The handbook advises new Germans to quickly learn the English language and find a job right away. Further, it suggests German immigrants take up lodging in a German boarding house as "indeed this seems to be preferable, for many reasons."

In addition, this handbook also placed an emphasis "on becoming a dutiful citizen, submitting cheerfully to the law, and taking a lively interest in America and its well-being," colorfully explaining that, "whoever wishes to be free, must not only eat the fruits of the tree of liberty, but also water its roots."

On January 19, 1876 the *S.S. Olbers* docked at the Washington Avenue Steamship Landing and Immigration Station in Philadelphia. Upon entering the city of Philadelphia, new immigrants would have sensed the historic ties of this city to Europe simply by walking its cobblestone streets and seeing its early colonial architecture. Horse and carriage services were available to shuttle passengers to nearby destinations, while various lines of the Pennsylvania Railroad were also within walking distance. These railroad lines transported new arrivals to further points within Philadelphia and across the country. But first, before one could roam freely, every new immigrant had to go through a lengthy customs process.

Prior to all ships arriving at their destination harbor, inspectors boarded the ship for cursory inspections. When the ship docked, all immigrants were examined by a doctor or nurse for injuries or illness. They were then processed by an inspector who reviewed their paperwork and usually asked them a series of questions. It was at this juncture that Jakob recounted one notable event.

As was customary, immigration officials commonly corrupted immigrant's names, either by misspelling accidentally or anglicizing it on purpose. Jakob noted that on all of his immigration papers, as well as the ship's manifest logs, his name had been changed to James. For the next fifty years in America Jakob would go by the name of James.

The final step of the customs process was the inspection of his baggage. After clearing customs, Jakob was able to go about and travel freely.

By the time Jakob arrived in America on that January day, Philadelphia was already astir and full of excitement, as the city was preparing to host America's Centennial Exhibition. The exhibition was scheduled to begin on April 19. Between his arrival in America and the start of the exhibition, Jakob recalled having plenty to do in preparation. But for now, having completed another portion of his memoir, Jakob tended to his sore throat in hopes of curing it.

CHAPTER 7

The Centennial Exhibition of 1876

People came from Europe and saw the future.
—George Thomas, historian, University of Pennsylvania on the Centennial Exhibition of 1876

On April 22, 1865, exactly one week after his assassination, Abraham Lincoln's body lay in state at Philadelphia's Independence Hall. For twenty-seven hours Philadelphians were allowed to pay their final respects and say their goodbyes to the man Ulysses S. Grant once called "the greatest man I ever knew."

Eleven bitter and angry years after Lincoln's death, Philadelphia became the city where signs of healing from the Civil War were first revealed to the rest of the world. In the same manner that Philadelphians unified to grieve the president's death, the Centennial Exhibition of 1876 would unify the North and the South as one nation.

The Centennial Exhibition was a celebration of the 100th anniversary of the American Revolution and the signing of the Declaration of Independence. This celebration was unique in that it was staged in the form of a world's fair, inviting natives and foreigners alike to take part.

The concept of a world exhibition was not new, as they dated back to 1851. In prior exhibitions, it was the responsibility of each host country's government to both organize and fund the event. Officials in the United States government were not excited when the idea was presented, however; they viewed it as a financially risky prospect and at first opposed the exhibition. It was not until Philadelphia's Select and Common Council (city council) proposed to put up most of the funds that the United States Congress finally agreed to pass a resolution to host the 1876 World Exhibition.

The Centennial Exhibition was the culmination of ten years of planning. It was initially conceived by Wabash College professor John Campbell, and the United States commissioner from the previous world's fair of 1871, Charles Norton. Both men believed that America's centennial was a milestone that deserved recognition. They envisioned an event that would not only be festive and memorable, but would also give visitors from around the world a glimpse of the tremendous growth and strides that America had made over the past one hundred years. In placing an emphasis on national progress, the Centennial Exhibition of 1876 became the greatest and most highly-attended extravaganza ever held in America's one-hundred year history. For this reason, the event became known as the crowning achievement of its time. In addition to all of America's thirty-seven states being represented, fifty separate countries also took part in the six-month festival.

JAKOB'S STORY AND THE AMERICAN DREAM

A few days had passed since Jakob had last worked on his memoir. His sore throat had worsened and he now had a low-grade fever to go along with the onset of the chills. In an attempt to fight the cold that was coming on, Jakob thought it best to get a couple of days' extra rest, thereby placing this project on a temporary hold. Then, having grown bored, but still feeling a bit under the weather, Jakob decided to return to working on his memoir. Jakob returned to his library and picked up writing where he had left off. Once again he drifted back to early 1876, retracing his steps when he first arrived in America. The memoir resumed by focusing on the days leading up to and his experience at the Centennial Exhibition.

With an immigration station located in its harbor, Philadelphia in the 1870s was a city of immigrants. By some estimates, one in every five residents was a new arrival. Often forgotten is the fact that it was a German immigrant, Hermann J. Schwarzmann, who was on the 1876 Centennial Commission and was almost exclusively responsible for the design of the entire 285-acre Centennial Exhibition fairgrounds, complete with its 250 pavilions.

Upon his arrival in Philadelphia, Jakob wasted no time in preparing for the exhibition's opening. Tasked with coordinating with the Deutz executives, Jakob was in charge of logistical details, such as having the various size engines shipped from Europe and transported to the fairgrounds. From there, other details, such as correctly arranging the engines in their display area, filled his time. Next, Jakob leased and opened a small office located at 119 South Fourth Street in Philadelphia so he could have a place to conduct business.

Two weeks before the exhibition was scheduled to open, additional help in the form of Jakob's younger brother, Adolph, arrived in America. Although the Centennial was initially scheduled to commence on April 19 in conjunction with the twenty-fifth anniversaries of the battles of Lexington and Concord, unexpected delays in construction pushed the starting date back three weeks to May 10. This delay allowed the Schleicher brothers extra time for preparation and a few days to simply take in the various sights in and around the city. In early May, Deutz's chief designer, Wilhelm Maybach, also arrived in America to assist the Schleichers in displaying the new "free piston engine."

Jakob recalled the festive atmosphere on the morning of May 10, 1876, as all of Philadelphia was about to proudly celebrate the commencement of the Centennial Exhibition. Just prior to the 10:30 AM opening, church bells could be heard across the city. The rain, which had been sprinkling all morning, stopped just as the opening ceremonies got underway. Following a brief remark by President Ulysses S. Grant and a 100-gun salute, the president, together with the emperor of Brazil, Don Pedro II, powered on a massive 650-ton, sixty-foot-tall Corliss Steam Engine to officially begin the start of this festival. This one Corliss engine powered virtually every exhibit at the fair.

Despite the fact that the Corliss Steam Engine was the darling of the exhibition, the steam engine industry entered a decline soon after. A brand new engine was about to make its debut in America.

With a great deal of pride for having played a special part in this key moment in America's industrial past, Jakob began to recount Eugen Langen's and Nicholas Otto's excitement as these men were given the opportunity to display their product to the American public for the first time. "The Centennial Exhibition of 1876 furnished them an exceptional opportunity to bring their engines before America. They [Langen and Otto] had prepared an elaborate exhibit."

JAKOB'S STORY AND THE AMERICAN DREAM

While the exhibition was divided into seven departments housed in five separate buildings, the entire 285-acre fairgrounds were alive with activity. Food vendors from around the world served various specialty foods. Novelty stands in the American section served "pop-corn" and "soda-water" while new consumable products such as "Hires" Root Beer, "Heintz" Ketchup and an exotic yellow fruit called a "banana," also made their debuts. In thinking of these various treats Jakob could recount their pleasant aromas and unique tastes even after all these years.

The exhibition was open six days a week (closed on Sundays). Attendees paid a sizeable fee—fifty cents—to tour the grounds and view new inventions such as the first Remington Typographic Machine (a.k.a. typewriter, complete with QWERTY keyboard) and the "Centennial Telephone Transmitter." Scottish immigrant Alexander Graham Bell had this intriguing device on display, amazing its audiences as it transmitted sounds over a wire. "My God, it talks!" Emperor Dom Pedro said as he held the receiver to his ear. This device was the precursor to the modern day telephone.

This World Exhibition, with its various demonstrations and exhibits, offered a hook for virtually every demographic in attendance. For women who toured the grounds there was a "colonial kitchen" complete with a spinning wheel, as well as docents who dressed in colonial era garb as they displayed what working in a kitchen was like during those early years.

For the youngest in attendance, watching the beautiful stallions in the Special Canadian Competition Horse Show brought considerable enjoyment. While a five-year-old stallion named Young Wonder won a gold medal, simply having the opportunity to watch these tame and elegant creatures was the greatest entertainment a child could imagine.

One young man in attendance, seventeen-year-old Frank L. Thomas, recorded his two-week visit to the Centennial from July 12-26, 1876 in his diary. A brief excerpt included the following entry:

> Friday, July 14th Arrived at the Centennial at 10:30. In United States Department – American Mechanical Warbles singing a sweet canary made by J. B. Cacor, Bridgeport, Conn. The renowned War Eagle Old Ben on exhibition. Old Abe was captured by Chippewa Indians on the Flambeau River, Wisconsin in the spring of 1861. Was sold to Company "C" 8th Wisconsin Regiment went to the front leading the war in march - was in 25 great battles in 3 years.

Statue of Liberty's arm bearing torch as it appeared on display at the 1876 Philadelphia Exhibition.

Gasmotorenfabrik Deutz display as it appeared at the 1876 Philadelphia Exhibition. Photo courtesy Hagley Museum.

The Centennial Exhibition was also where Americans got their first glimpse of Eduardo Laboulaye's and Frederic-Auguste Bartholdi's monument of independence. The hand bearing the torch of the Statue of Liberty was on display. For an additional fifty cents, visitors could climb up a ladder inside the arm to the torch's balcony where they got a clear view of the entire Fairmount Park fairgrounds. Describing the overall experience at the exhibition, and taking special note of the Statue of Liberty's meaning, University of Pennsylvania historian George Thomas remarked, "People came from Europe and saw the future."

The second largest building on the fairgrounds was Machinery Hall. It displayed a wide assortment of every conceivable machine possible. The centerpiece was the enormous Corliss

Steam Engine. James D. McCabe, in his 1876 commemorative book, *The Illustrated History of the Centennial Exhibition*, described Machinery Hall thus: "Along the south aisle several gas-engines of a peculiar construction are in operation, showing how a steady motive power is derived from the explosive force of ordinary burning gas. They are exhibited by the Gas Motor Factory, of Deutz." Seven various sized motors produced by the German company Gasmotorenfabrik Deutz, (Gas Engine Factory of Deutz) were on display in this building. Although these engines drew much curiosity, America was deeply entrenched with their steam engines at the time. To most visitors a gas-powered engine seemed not only foreign, but impractical. While Otto's free piston engine did receive a fair amount of publicity in American newspapers and periodicals, it was not always positive.

On June 29, 1876, the *New York Times* published a rather perplexing article about this new engine. "In the Prussian section of this department are several small engines of a somewhat novel construction, which appear to be rather a vexed question among the mechanical visitors to the Exhibition. They are the small Atmospheric Gas Engines exhibited by Langen and Otto." Following a description of how the engine operates, the article marginally acknowledged their usefulness. "These engines form an interesting exhibit, and have always a crowd of admirers or engineers around them," the article concludes.

Clearly referencing the downward pounding motion and excessive noise that this early gas engine produced, the July 1, 1876 issue of *Scientific American* described it, condescendingly, as a "gunpowder pile-driver."

Perhaps it was a result of the negative press reports, or the engine's excessive noise. Maybe it was America's overall lack of familiarity with a gas-powered engine, or a combination of all of these factors, but as the exhibition moved into the later summer months, sales of the Otto Free Piston Engine were virtually nonexistent.

Sitting in his library that quiet morning, Jakob momentarily paused from typing. Almost fifty years had passed since the Centennial Exhibition had taken place. After all this time, Jakob still could not comprehend America's overall lack of interest in the gas engine in those early days. On his typewriter he continued: "It was admitted by the inventors that the Langen and Otto engine was noisy, but should this have debarred the engine from any sale whatever here when thousands of them were sold elsewhere on account of many evident and excellent qualities?"

The 1876 Exhibition continued through the remainder of the summer. The heat wave, which topped 100 degrees several times in June and July, did not deter visitors from attending in the late summer, as evident by the record crowd of 274,919 that arrived on September 28. Clearly however, there was a level of disappointment with Otto and Langen's Atmospheric Gas Engine. When word got back to Eugen Langen and Nicholas Otto at the Deutz Factory in Germany about the engine's poor performance, they decided a remedy for its excessive noise had to be addressed immediately. With their chief designer away in America, Deutz turned to a newly hired engineer, Hermann Schumm, to help find a solution to the engine's lackluster performance.

Thirty-five-year-old Hermann Schumm had an impressive résumé. Having worked two years as a technical designer for the Karlsruhe engine company, Schumm also taught mechanical engineering for two years at a vocational school in Basel. In addition, Hermann Schumm worked three years as an advanced engineer for the Birnbacher company. His first task working for Deutz was to assist Nicholas Otto in creating a newer, quieter four-stroke engine.

Just as the exhibition was winding down, a breakthrough took place at the Deutz factory. Jakob recounted the excitement on that November day in 1876 when he received the news. Nicholas Otto and Hermann Schumm had created a smoother, more powerful, efficient and quieter "four-stroke silent engine." Within days of its first test, the following telegram arrived in Philadelphia from his Uncle Eugen:

> For the first time last night the 8 horse-power ran so elegantly and beautifully that it must have been joy for the angels.

The contents of this one telegram provided the Schleicher brothers the motivation and excitement they needed to carry on their work in America.

As he had earlier reflected on touring the field of battle at Waterloo, Jakob spent a few moments thinking about his experience at the Centennial Exhibition of 1876. Jakob realized in retrospect that this event was more than just a world's fair or a consumer showcase. It had undoubtedly pitted innovators, industrialists and entrepreneurs against each other in a battle of industrial supremacy. But it had also shown consumers what technology in a modern world looked like, and in some sense, it refined urban life. Consumer outlets began appearing shortly after the exhibition ended. But the 1876 Centennial was even more than all of this. Jakob realized that America was an idea. He saw this country as having a spirit of enterprise. It was the place where people from anywhere could converge with ideas and an adventurous spirit and make something of themselves.

JAKOB'S STORY AND THE AMERICAN DREAM

Thinking about the Statue of Liberty's torch when it was first on display, Jakob saw this torch figuratively lighting a path toward the modern world. For although his American Dream had not yet been fully realized in 1876, his dream had been set in motion. While there were trials and much hard work still ahead, he would soon find happiness, prosperity and success. With that in mind, Jakob set himself to plunge ahead writing, and to persevere when it came time to describe the clouds of fate that formed on the distant horizon after his arrival in America.

CHAPTER 8

Schleicher, Schumm & Company

Before anything else, preparation is the key to success.
— Alexander Graham Bell

Now Jakob's fever, chills and fatigue were only made worse by the fact that he had no one to help nurse him back to health. Still, he managed to sit at his desk for short periods each day, writing about the events that followed the 1876 Centennial Exhibition.

It was at this juncture, as Jakob was reflecting on his past, that he remembered something Alexander Graham Bell had said while introducing his Centennial Telephone Transmitter at the exhibition. "Before anything else, preparation is the key to success," Bell explained. Jakob decided this theme would drive the next part of his memoir.

One key to Jakob's success in America came in the form of Deutz's newest employee, Hermann Schumm, who, following his initial assignment aiding Nicholas Otto in creating a new and improved engine, was chosen in late 1877 to be Wilhelm Maybach's replacement in America. With his firsthand working knowledge of the new Otto Four Stroke Engine, as well as his ability to teach, Schumm became the perfect candidate to send to Philadelphia. Jakob then began to sketch out his impressions of Mr. Schumm.

Jakob Schleicher's business partner and brother-in-law, Hermann Schumm.

JAKOB'S STORY AND THE AMERICAN DREAM

Upon Hermann Schumm's arrival in America, Jakob was immediately impressed with his ability to simplify and articulate the purpose for each part of an engine, the engine's assembly and the mechanics by which it operated. On a personal level, Jakob remembered Schumm's very patient and outgoing disposition; he was naturally suited to be an instructor. Jakob and Adolph embraced their new associate and treated him as if he were a long-lost brother. Hermann Schumm also took a liking to the Schleichers. As a tribute, and as a gesture of goodwill and acceptance, the Schleicher brothers changed the name of their business to Schleicher, Schumm & Company to include the newest member of their team.

Jakob then recounted how a turning point occurred in the gas engine industry, taking place over roughly the same two-year span as Hermann Schumm's stay in America. Jakob's memoir noted that although sales of the new and improved "silent engine" were still sparse, America's view of gas-powered engines had reached a tipping point.

"The gas-engine in public favor was very slow, so that from May 1877, to May 1879, in two years not quite 30 engines had been placed," Jakob wrote. Competing against the well-established steam engine, along with its price and limited availability of gasoline, became the major hindrances that kept consumers away. "So little use did the American people seem to have for a noisy motor, however safe and clean, but consuming the expensive commodity of illuminating (non-liquid) gas, which rated from $2.15 [per 100 cubic feet] in Philadelphia...and in small towns [up] to $5.00 [per 100 cubic feet]" was clearly a hurdle most consumers avoided all together," Jakob recalled. "The American market was a law to itself and a foothold could only be gained by slow degrees," he explained.

Then, a year and a half into Hermann Schumm's visit to America, the great gas engine experiment made its first solid step forward. In late 1878, as the senior partner in the firm, Jakob traveled to New York to attend the American Gas Light Association's annual meeting. It was there that interest in the Otto Gas Engine first gained recognition. America was about to embrace the Otto Engine in earnest.

At this meeting Jakob was interviewed about the new Otto Engine. Jakob spoke confidently about the future of this engine, and those in attendance seemed to gravitate toward his energetic and upbeat attitude. Jakob first pointed out that, unlike the steam engine, the Otto Engine was clean and could be used indoors. Emphasizing the engine's high quality workmanship, he made sure to say that these state-of-the-art machines were priced the same as the steam engine at the competitive mark of only $400. Jakob also used the meeting as a platform to explain the technical aspects of how the engine operated. Going over the various integral parts, including the induction system, cylinder heads, its piston, camshaft and flywheel, Jakob noted that each part was handcrafted to precision and designed to operate in sync with each other. As such, his product was the most efficient machine available to the public.

Jakob explained the principles and concept of the engine in a step-by-step fashion to members of the association. These steps included the induction stroke, the compression stroke, the expansion stroke and the exhaust stroke. In simplified terms the four-step process operated in the following manner:

The first step in the process was the induction stroke. During this initial phase a mixture of fuel and air was drawn into the combustion chamber.

During the second step a "carrier flame" contained within the thickness of the slide valve was generated in the piston, thereby initiating the combustion of the fuel.

The third step used the expanded gas to propel the piston, thus creating the force necessary to drive the connecting mechanism.

In the fourth and final step the combusted fuel traveled to the exhaust valve. Continuing its discharge from the engine, this expended gas traveled through and exited the exhaust manifold pipe. The four steps would then repeat in the same cycle.

Although his explanation was not as eloquent as perhaps Mr. Schumm's could have been, Jakob's presentation laid out in great detail all of the potential benefits of this engine. He explained that, even with higher fuel prices, the Otto Four Stroke Engine was more cost efficient than the traditional steam engine. Factoring in the total cost of operating the Otto Engine, including maintenance and cleaning as well as its handling cost of only 4.5 cents per hour per indicated horsepower, the benefit of owning this engine was well worth its investment. Unable to debate its efficiency or its low cost to operate, the members of the association were astounded by this engine's qualities. Now, for the first time since its introduction in America two and a half years earlier, the gas engine was afforded serious consideration. Shortly after this gathering, word began to slowly trickle out about this remarkable engine. Soon the Otto Engine began receiving positive publicity in American periodicals.

Jakob arose from his desk and walked to a file cabinet in the corner of his library. Opening a drawer, he removed an envelope containing newspaper clippings and various articles he had saved over the years about the Otto Engine. Returning to his desk he opened the envelope and transcribed relevant pieces from two articles into his memoir.

An article from the December 21, 1878 issue of *Scientific American* highlighted the engine's predominant selling features. They included the overall safety and lack of attention needed while the engine was in use, the engine's constant readiness, its ability to start instantly, and how all expenses ceased when the engine stopped. A follow-up article in the March 29, 1879 issue stated that the Otto Four Stroke Engine was "the only economical and practical gas engine in the market." Jakob then noted that, within weeks of this second article, the Otto Engine's sales quickly spiked as a new utility had emerged in America: the arc-electric light.

"1879 and 1880 marked the beginning of the electric era and brought quite some excitement to the gas-man and gas stock holder," Jakob remembered. "The gas engine became at once a subject of intense interest and the whole gas fraternity and the manufacturers in Philadelphia (Schleicher, Schumm & Company) were glad of the opportunity," Jakob proudly recalled.

Upon completion of his two-year commitment in America, Hermann Schumm returned to Europe and married one of Jakob and Adolph's younger sisters. Now a brother-in-law, Schumm was reassigned to the Deutz French affiliate in Paris. He and Jakob kept in regular contact with each other until Schumm's death in 1901. But now, reflecting back all these years later, Jakob had not only come to realize the value of their friendship, but he also had a deeper appreciation for the contributions Schumm had made in making Jakob's business venture in America successful.

After concluding this portion of his memoir, Jakob left his library and went to make a telephone call. Up to this point Jakob had been ill for almost two weeks. With his cold continuing to linger and not improve, he decided to telephone his physician.

Physicians regularly made residential "house calls" in the nineteenth century and early twentieth century. For multiple reasons during this period, going to the family doctor's office was a difficult and sometimes impossible task for many. Transportation was not always reliable or available, and there was no emergency response system in place. Moreover, the lack of smooth asphalt-sealed roads meant that moving ill patients could be risky. Thus, house calls were in most instances the only practical means of treating the sick during this period of American history.

Equipped with a hinged leather bag known as a Gladstone bag, a general practitioner would arrive at a patient's home with a variety of medical equipment, ready to handle virtually any kind of medical emergency. The medical bag routinely included medicines, thermometers, stethoscopes, syringes and even surgery kits. General practitioners were medical doctors with a general knowledge in all fields of human anatomy, able to perform virtually every sort of medical procedure.

Upon arriving at Jakob's home the next day, the doctor took note of the cleanliness of his patient's abode and Jakob's kempt appearance. The doctor observed his patient's mobility: fully able to move and get around, slow due to loss of muscle tone and balance but rather normal for a person of his age. The doctor's cursory exam of Jakob included noting the following symptoms: cough, runny nose, a slight fever and fatigue. The good doctor prescribed his patient additional rest, fluids to avoid dehydration, and a recheck in two weeks. Hesitantly, Jakob agreed to use the next couple of weeks to rest before engaging in any arduous or laborious work. A few days later Jakob returned to his library and resumed work on his memoir.

Otto Gas Engines powering Philadelphia's Central Station, circa 1880s.

Following Shumm's return to Europe, production and sales of Otto's silent engine steadily increased at the Schleicher, Schumm & Company factory in Philadelphia. "In the year 1880, the output of the Philadelphia works rose to about 200 engines, in 1881 to 300, and in 1882 to 500 engines," Jakob wrote. With production numbers on the rise and with a higher volume of business, Schleicher, Schumm & Company relocated to a newer, larger, four-story factory. Not surprisingly, the company's pride in their precision work carried over into their new facility, as Jakob's clip from the periodical *Steven Indicator* illustrated:

"One would notice immediately the exceptional cleanliness of the interior, also the neat fresh appearance of the exterior of the building, and that order and system reigned supreme."

But even this new facility was not without its own set of problems. Although the new factory was constructed with well over one hundred windows, during the hot Philadelphia summers, inside this brick building temperatures became unbearable, commonly reaching over ninety degrees. With no insulation or heating, the 300 employees working in this factory fared no better during the winter. Snow outside brought the inside temperatures down into the forties. Additionally, employees would commonly strain their eyes due to the dim indoor lighting.

Engine production began with a four horsepower engine. Within a few months, two and seven horsepower versions were introduced. Within the next few years, sizes were available up to fifty horsepower. The engines produced at this factory were used for a variety of tasks including hoisting, pumping, ventilating, and powering various pieces of electrical machinery. Ironically, the most common use of these engines was as a dynamo for electric lighting. Buried deep inside the manila envelope where Jakob kept the news clippings, he found a letter from one New Orleans business owner who sent in the following testimonial to the Schleicher & Schumm Company, dated in 1881:

"The seven-horse-power new Otto Silent Gas Engine gives perfect satisfaction in its performance. The simplicity, safety, and cleanliness of the engine are some of the great merits to make it preferable to any other motor."

Large entities had begun purchasing the Otto Engine from Schleicher & Schumm, including numerous city utility departments that used these engines to power city street lamps during evening hours. The United States government also purchased a large number of these engines to use in the arsenal at Watertown, Massachusetts.

By the 1880s the Otto Engine had become the standard of comparison for all engines manufactured in America. As Jakob noted, "It was our object to build an engine as near faultless as possible." But, while this decade had brought a level of professional success, Jakob was unprepared for the various changes that were about to take place at home and abroad during this same period.

Within every organization there are many moving parts. When all of these parts are moving in the same direction, order, structure and a day-to-day functionality are created. At the same time, it is every organization's goal to finely tune various aspects of its operation in order to find their peak level of success. In this respect, Gasmotorenfabrik Deutz was no different from any other company, past or present. Sometimes, however, favors within an organization are granted to help with achieving this goal. In Deutz's case, favors within the organization brought about disagreement, strife and ultimately irreconcilable differences.

As far back as 1872, some business decisions made during the expansion and incorporation of the Gasmotorenfabrik Deutz, later led to conflict. For example, while Eugen Langen's siblings invested capital into the business, Nicholas Otto did not. Although Nicholas Otto was well compensated financially and held a seat in the board of directors, he held less clout in the company and was easily outvoted by the Langen family members on the board.

The circumstances of Gottlieb Daimler's hiring was also a sore point. Daimler, with his university background and prior upper management history, insisted, as a condition of his employment, that he be given a position within the firm equivalent to Nicholas Otto's. When Eugen Langen conceded this request, it ultimately set the stage for a major conflict between the main

JAKOB'S STORY AND THE AMERICAN DREAM

associates of the company. The tension between formally educated Daimler and autodidact Nicholas Otto surfaced slowly. In the beginning, Daimler demanded separate housing facilities. Disagreements later developed about financial compensation and entitlements, and overflowed into new production ideas and other technical improvements. Both men seemed determined to butt heads with each other.

In December 1881, Gottlieb Daimler was dismissed from Deutz. Following Wilhelm Maybach's departure in April 1882, these two longtime friends joined together as business partners. They created a smaller, lighter and faster version of the four-stroke engine, which achieved a remarkable speed of 600 RPM. In comparison, Deutz industrial engines still chugged along at only 120 to 180 RPM. In November 1885 Daimler and Maybach used their "simplified" engine to create the world's first riding carriage, called the Reitwagen, later known as the motorcycle.

By this time, patent fights began to surface among Deutz and its competing manufacturers. In 1884 a seemingly weak case was submitted to the German courts claiming that a French pamphlet detailing the concept of the Otto Four Stroke Cycle predated the first engine Nicholas Otto had built. When the courts failed to rule in Deutz's favor, all of Nicholas Otto's German patents were promptly revoked, leaving the Deutz company with no form of recourse or appeal. By 1886 anyone in Germany could legally manufacture and sell the Otto Four Stroke Engine.

After years of haggling internally with Gottlieb Daimler and losing his patent rights, the stress and tension finally caught up with Nicholas Otto. Worn out by all the strain, Otto suffered a heart attack in January 1891. The man whose invention first paved the way for Jakob's voyage to America died at the age of fifty-eight.

All of these managerial and legal changes wearied Eugen Langen as well. While the new developments did not directly affect the Philadelphia manufacturing plant, the following turn of events had a much more direct impact on Jakob, both personally and professionally.

Jakob remembered wistfully that the mid-1880s were becoming a difficult period for his business partner and brother, Adolph. Adolph and his wife, Anna, were both having difficulty adjusting to the hot Philadelphia summers. Adolph started suffering from the long term effects of sunstroke, while Anna lost two consecutive children during pregnancy. In an effort to improve his family's health, Adolph began taking his wife and children on trips back to the much cooler climate of Europe. With a business to operate in America, however, these trips were always short-lived. With his medical conditions worsening, Adolph found it difficult to concentrate and no longer enjoyed the same level of satisfaction his work had once given him. For all the success that had come to Adolph over these past several years, doubts began to surface whether Philadelphia was the right place for him and his family.

Adolph Schleicher Jr. Photo courtesy: Chronicle of the Langen Family Assn.

JAKOB'S STORY AND THE AMERICAN DREAM

By June 1889 Adolph had reached a life changing decision: he was selling his portion of the business and permanently returning to Europe with his family. A deeply devout Reformed Protestant, Adolph was intent on devoting the rest of his life to missionary work. In preparation for his calling, Adolph decided to move his family to Berlin, Germany, where he could return to school.

As if the departure of his brother wasn't difficult enough to deal with, another shift in technology was also beginning to take place. This evolving technology had the potential to affect Jakob's entire livelihood. In his memoir he recalled:

> The electric companies had started with first robbing gas companies of their street lighting contracts, supplying arc-lighting; a few years later the bid for domestic and store lighting, using the incandescent light; at last, with the perfection of the electric motor and of their devices for reliability carrying power currents, an attack was made on our gas power.

Competition between gas power and electricity put Jakob at risk of losing a large portion of his business. He knew the battle would be decided by one simple factor: which utility would be cheaper for consumers in the long run? Unfortunately for Jakob, the question was answered sooner rather than later. He reasoned,

> Had gas companies fought for [lower prices] years ago and brought the same sacrifices as their electric rivals, these latter [electric companies] would not have made the rapid progress they did, as gas under a continuous production could have been sold at less cost than electric companies can afford to sell day-current, and these

would have had hardly any inducements to attack gas power. As a result of this, the output of gas engines fell off materially at that time (1889–1891) and recovered only very slowly in subsequent years.

Then, as if it had just occurred yesterday, Jakob documented one of his life's most painful episodes. It began May 2, 1894 when Eugen Langen received an urgent telegram at the company headquarters in Germany. It caught him and everyone else at Deutz off guard. After reading the telegram, Eugen must have felt that this message needed to be delivered in person and immediately made arrangements to travel to Philadelphia in what would become his only trip to America. Nine days later, Eugen's ship docked in New York. During the entire journey to Philadelphia, Eugen worried over how to break this news to Jakob.

Jakob no doubt wondered what had brought his uncle all the way from Germany to America. Their exchange was sobering.

Unable to come up with the right words to tell his nephew, Eugen Langen handed Jakob the same telegram he had received the week prior. Jakob remembered his heart pounding as he began reading the telegram, his expression blank. For a moment, time stopped. Jakob's brother, Adolph, who had left Philadelphia to get away from the warm climate in America, had died on the way to Tanzania before he could fulfill his vocation as a missionary there. Eugen filled in the details not included in the telegram.

Six days into his fourteen-day voyage from Germany to Tanzania, Adolph was stricken with a fever, followed by a bout of seasickness and dysentery. Probably unaware of its severity, Adolph had contracted tropical fever. Without the aid of a doctor or proper medication on board the ship, his fever became more violent and severe. His condition worsened and his health rapidly deteriorated. Unconsciousness quickly set in, followed by death.

Devastated and overcome with emotion, Jakob was momentarily speechless.

After the initial shock wore off, he and his Uncle Eugen, now age sixty-one, had a heart-to-heart talk. Similar to when Eugen asked Jakob to travel to America, Eugen had another offer to present to his nephew. This time he offered to purchase Jakob's affiliated American branch of Deutz. Eugen was tired. The lawsuits brought about by Deutz's competitors over patent rights and the internal conflicts had taken their toll. Before anything happened to him, Eugen wanted to ensure his nephew was fully compensated for all of his efforts. As far as Eugen was concerned, the great experiment was over and Jakob had honorably completed all that was asked of him.

Jakob agreed. Having dedicated nearly two decades to the company, Jakob was emotionally exhausted. In selling his portion of the business, Jakob retired from the role of vice-president with a comfortable severance package of half a million dollars.

On July 5, 1894 Schleicher, Schumm & Company was quickly renamed the Otto Gas Engine Works. Under new management, it became the American counterpart to the German company, Deutz. One year later Eugen Langen died in Cologne, Germany of heart failure.

Jakob ended this portion of his memoir as he typed the following:

> The gas-engine was put on American soil, as an exotic plant born abroad and grown under the sunshine of cheap gas. The Otto [Engine] had a hardy nature, which at first merely allowed it to sustain life unsupported,

then grew stronger and survived long enough until the climatic conditions necessary for its prosperity changed. The gas industry of the country will be the most important and permanent beneficiary by the growth of gas-power in the future, as it has been in the past, and it is important that it should be fully aware of this fact.

As Jakob thought about his days working as an engineer and those relationships that had come and gone over the years, he also began thinking about other people with whom he had developed friendships. Manufacturing and selling engines in America was rewarding, but as he reflected on those who meant the most to him, he knew the next chapter was going to be devoted to those special relationships he had cultivated during his time in America.

CHAPTER 9

A Twist of Fate

It was written I should be loyal to the nightmare of my choice.
—Joseph Conrad, Heart of Darkness

Over the past fifty years America had provided Jakob many opportunities. These opportunities included freedom, liberty, living the American Dream and achieving a measureable amount of success. But of all these opportunities, perhaps the most meaningful were the various relationships Jakob had cultivated. Jakob noticed that, while each relationship was meaningful in its own special way, it was the few close friendships that had become the most pivotal parts of his life in America. Oddly, Jakob thought, his closest and longest lasting relationships were the ones cultivated upon his arrival to Philadelphia in 1876.

Following the advice in the handbook, *The German in America*, shortly after arriving in Philadelphia, Jakob began searching for a German-speaking household where he could stay as a boarder. Many new immigrants felt boarding with an established immigrant family was a prudent first step upon arriving in America. For most immigrants, having someone who spoke their same tongue and were familiar with the new area and new customs brought a level of comfort and reassurance. Additionally, most newcomers usually gravitated to established areas in America where European natives who shared their same origin built tight-knit communities. People looked after each other and schooled the new arrivals in local customs and practical matters. Boarding thus became commonplace during the nineteenth century. Two well-established German communities in Philadelphia were known as Germantown and Strawberry Mansion.

Germantown was located in northwestern Philadelphia; Strawberry Mansion was north of the city. Both of these neighborhoods consisted of two- and three-story, single-family colonial and Victorian style homes. Jakob located a boardinghouse that bordered on the Strawberry Mansion district, near his newly established office. He chose to rent a room from August and Elvina Ebeling, a German couple who themselves had immigrated to America from Hannover, Germany back in the 1850s.

Upon arriving in America, August Ebeling made his living as a cigar salesman and married Elvina Hewel in 1866. The newlyweds relocated from New York to Philadelphia in the 1860s where they had one son, Adolph. To supplement their family income, this couple rented out spare rooms of their home to travelers and boarders. When Jakob met August Ebeling, their German background became the foundation of their friendship. It was also during Jakob's stay with the Ebelings that he met the woman he would come to love for the rest of his days—the couple's niece, Elvina Baron.

As a result of serious differences between Elvina Baron and her mother, the Ebelings opened their home to their niece in

JAKOB'S STORY AND THE AMERICAN DREAM

1881. Elvina Baron was an attractive, warm, cheerful and prudent woman. Jakob took an instant liking to the Ebelings' attractive niece, whose charismatic personality made her warm and pleasant to be around. Soon after, Elvina Baron began reciprocating Jakob's feelings. A force seemingly stronger than chance had apparently destined these two lives to cross paths. Before long, however, destiny would also take a strange twist for these two.

Now twenty-nine years old and having been in America for five years, Jakob had familiarized himself with his surroundings and accustomed himself to America's culture and way of life. Overall, he was comfortable in his environment, but there were a few social rules whose full importance he hadn't yet grasped.

Just as he began giving an account of an episode that took place one morning in the summer of 1881, there was a knock at the front door. For a moment Jakob was undecided. Should he continue typing and avoid losing his train of thought, or should he answer the door? Alone at home during the day, Jakob was unaccustomed to having visitors come to the door like this. As the knocking became harder and louder Jakob slowly made his way to the front door. Pleased to discover his nephew Lewis Mumford had dropped in for a visit, Jakob blithely allowed his guest inside.

Lewis Mumford had a unique relationship with his Uncle Jakob. Lewis remembered how his uncle began encouraging him to read at an early age, regularly gifting him various forms of literature. But in addition to remembering his uncle passing along his voracious interest in reading, Lewis also recounted how his Uncle Jakob also tried to subtly influence him via the type of literature he gave him to read. "My uncle Jakob, he had been trained in the classics and had a true taste for literature: it was he who gave me Viktor von Scheffel's *Ekkehard* to counterbalance the picture of the Middle Ages I had found in Walter Scott," wrote Mumford. There were numerous other instances in the past in which Jakob attempted to sway his nephew's views. Nevertheless, during the infrequent times they met, Mumford deeply enjoyed visiting his uncle. "The more my mind developed, the closer we found ourselves when we met," Mumford warmly remembered.

Over a cup of coffee, the two shared current events in their lives. Lewis told his uncle about the birth of his first child, a son named Geddes, who was now six months old. Lewis also talked about his recent trip to Switzerland and the progress he was making on his third book, *The Golden Day: A Study in American Experience and Culture*. As a sociologist and literary critic, Lewis was fascinated with urban architecture. In his upcoming book, Lewis captured America's transition circa 1830–1860 from an early settlement into a society of capitalism. Lewis dubbed this thirty-year span the "golden day." Lewis shared with his uncle how he believed during the golden day there was a fine balance between two economies, agriculture and industry, either of which could become the climax of the American experience. Following this period was America's Civil War, followed by industrialism and a dominating philosophy of pragmatism, which, in Lewis' opinion, signaled America's decline.

Jakob, on the other hand, spoke of his current project of writing a memoir. This project was Jakob's way of occupying these empty days by writing about his most memorable experiences, giving meaning to them and allowing him to reflect back on his life's journey one more time. As Jakob shared with his nephew, Lewis began to take notice of his uncle's cold symptoms: a hoarse and dry cough, alternating pale and flush skintones, as

JAKOB'S STORY AND THE AMERICAN DREAM

well as a tired and worn out appearance. Although what he saw troubled him, Lewis encouraged his uncle to continue writing and to get plenty of rest.

Their visit lasted around two hours. When it was time for Lewis to go, Jakob thanked his nephew for taking the time to check up on him. Lewis, in turn, requested that his uncle take care of his cold. Both then wished each other well and promised to see each other again soon. As his nephew departed, Jakob came to the realization that *this* is what he had desired from long ago. It had been years since he had shared a meaningful conversation, where companionship warmed his sense of kinship. Where he was not only heard and deeply understood, but also cared for. Much like enjoying dinner at a fine dining establishment, this visit had in fact become food for Jakob's soul.

A couple of days passed before Jakob once again returned to his memoir. His visit with nephew Lewis Mumford, while pleasant, had also brought to the surface the single most disappointing and painful episode of his life. Incidentally, this also happened to be the exact point where Jakob had stopped typing earlier, and where he was set to resume working on his memoir. As he had grown accustomed to doing, Jakob once again returned to the library and powered on his radiola, and began typing.

It was a Saturday morning in the summer of 1881. While August and Elvina Ebeling had left for some errands, their niece, Elvina Baron, and Jakob were alone in the house. It began innocently enough, with Jakob and Miss Baron talking in the living room. As their conversation intensified, Jakob casually began shortening the distance between them. Soon the two were standing next to each other. Then, Jakob gently pulled her toward him and tenderly placed a kiss on her lips. "I do no more remember what our conversation was but I was so drawn to her that I could not help placing a chaste kiss on her lips. She accepted it as a natural tribute due her, not worth any comments either to myself or to her aunt or uncle upon their return," Jakob reflected. Instantly the two fell in love.

Sitting in his library that winter morning, Jakob noted that forty-five years had passed since that kiss took place. He stood by his original position: that nothing more was intended that day than a chaste but affectionate kiss. Unfortunately for Jakob and Miss Baron, the woman of the house did not share these same sentiments. It would not be until years later that Jakob learned how soon after, Elvina Baron naïvely told her aunt that the handsome, blue-eyed boarder had kissed her. Aunt Elvina reacted with indignation.

In that era women were generally held accountable for men's judgment lapses regarding physical intimacy. For Jakob's part, he probably knew that, while Miss Baron's womanly charms beguiled him, the choice to act on his feelings was a poor one. He took advantage of the fact that no one else was home. Even giving Jakob the benefit of the doubt—he may not have been *fully* aware that he had committed a social infraction—he had nonetheless violated this family's household rules. As a paying guest, however, Jakob was not the one who received punishment.

Believing that her niece had committed a grave breach of the family's household rules, Elvina Ebeling came up with a solution. The following Monday, after Jakob left to go to work, she promptly sent her niece back home to New York. Being thus shamed and having to depart so abruptly, crushed young Elvina, and was no doubt painful for Jakob as well. Left in an odd predicament, Jakob made no attempt to contact Elvina, fearing that asking the Ebelings for a forwarding address might result in his own dismissal from their home. By this time Jakob could afford his own lodging, but he also valued the Ebelings' friendship. Therefore, with their new romance quickly terminated and with no means of contacting each other, any hopes of these two having a future together seemed rather bleak. Regretfully, Jakob and Elvina Baron moved on with their lives, always left to wonder what could have been. For Jakob, the end of this courtship stung all the more when he learned his brother Adolph and his wife, who had married the year prior, were expecting the birth of their first child.

Not long after this incident, tragedy struck the Ebeling family.

Without warning August Ebeling, who had become Jakob's close friend, suffered a devastating back injury. Paraplegia rapidly took August's ability to use his lower extremities. Complications followed, and August's health quickly deteriorated. Within a few weeks, forty-seven-year-old August Ebeling succumbed to his injuries. His untimely death created a vacuum in the Ebeling home as the main source of this family's income was suddenly gone.

Now a widow, Elvina Ebeling was devastated. She immediately began to worry over such matters as what might happen if one of the boarders moved out of her home. Where would she come up with the monthly income to put food on the table and pay the utilities? Lost and heartbroken, she worried about these issues, as did her now nineteen-year-old son, Adolph. In addition to these concerns, Adolph worried about his mother's well-being. The idea that he would now be financially responsible for supporting his mother for an indefinite time consumed him. Mother and son fell into an overwhelming tailspin.

At the time of August Ebeling's death, life insurance in America had been available to the public for over 100 years. In 1760 the Presbyterian Synod of Philadelphia became the first company to offer life insurance in America. This was followed in 1875 when the Widows and Orphans Friendly Society (later renamed the Prudential Life Insurance Company) was founded in New Jersey. This company was the first to offer burial insurance. Unfortunately for the Ebeling family, they had never engaged in estate planning nor bought insurance. They had nothing set aside for burial expenses either.

Elvina Ebeling and her son Adolph were now, like many widowed families of the period, forced to use their home as their only form of income. The boardinghouse still did not bring in enough revenue each month to cover their expenses. Having lived with the family for a number of years, Jakob was keenly aware that the dynamics had changed.

In an effort to help the Ebelings, Jakob hired Adolph to work as a clerk at the Schleicher & Schumm factory. It was something, but was still not a long-term solution to their financial dilemma.

Elvina Ebeling was a sensitive, sympathetic, highly intelligent woman who had a passion for cleanliness. After her husband's death her tendency to be over censorious about the moral standards of those around her worsened and she became increasingly needy of affirmation and security. One year after her husband's death, Elvina Ebeling turned fifty years old. She obsessed over her financial future. Her son's new employment with Schleicher & Schumm's engine factory seemed promising, but it would be some time before his income could do more than barely supplement what she collected from boarders. Moreover, she didn't want to burden her son down the road, when he might marry and have a family of his own. She must have wondered: *Who would marry a woman of my age?* She began to see her boarder, Jakob Schleicher, as a convenient choice. After all, she reasoned, she had known him for several years and he had a stable job with a good income.

Out of concern for Elvina and Adolph Ebeling's circumstances, and realizing that at age forty his window of opportunity to marry and begin a family was closing, Jakob agreed to marry this widow. Their wedding took place on December 12, 1892. While the marriage made sense on many levels, it came with emotional ties, namely to Elvina Baron. Deep down, Jakob was still conflicted. Having never lost the feelings he had for Elvina, he mourned the loss of the future he had once dreamed of spending with her. All these years later Jakob admitted that the image of Miss Baron had haunted him throughout his married life. Following her marriage to Jakob, Elvina once again resumed kindly relations with her niece.

**Elvina (Baron) Mumford and Lewis Mumford.
Photo courtesy Carol Huber Roper.**

After learning of Jakob's marriage to her aunt in 1892, Elvina Baron quickly married too. After giving birth to a son, her relationship soured and came to an abrupt end. For years Jakob pondered if this child was a subtle message and a lasting reminder to him of what he did not have, or rather, what he could have had if he married Elvina Baron instead of choosing the less-risky option of staying in Philadelphia and overseeing the Schleicher & Schumm engine factory. As it so happened, because of her age, Jakob's wife never bore Jakob a child, and Elvina Baron's son was Lewis Mumford.

A line from a book Jakob had recently finished reading came to mind. It fittingly summarized this episode of his life. From Joseph Conrad's *Heart of Darkness* Jakob quoted: "It was written I should be loyal to the nightmare of my choice." He remained loyal to his choices, albeit with mixed emotions.

Following his marriage in 1892 and the subsequent sale of his portion of the engine factory a year and a half later, Jakob recalled feeling that change was on the horizon. As the nineteenth century came to a close with a new century preparing to begin, new paths and opportunities were about to open, not just for Jakob, but for American society as a whole.

CHAPTER 10

Industrialism, Progressivism and a Brief Retirement

The Arrival of a New Era is Felt and Not Measured.
—Walter Lord, author

As the Gilded Age was winding down from about 1894 to 1900, both America and Jakob Schleicher experienced a time of transition. The impact of this era could be felt in virtually every aspect of American life. The gas engines Jakob's factory produced had brought about a number of drastic changes. For example, it was the first time in history that people had the ability to work during the evening hours. This was a direct result of gas-powered engines being used as dynamos to run the earliest form of electricity, the arc-electric light. Next, these same dynamos powered large-scale electrical infrastructure, as city streetlights were illuminated during evening hours, bringing a new level to public safety. But perhaps the single most significant advancement of the nineteenth century was a direct offshoot of Nicholas Otto's gas engine — the automobile.

The changes that had come about in America just since Jakob's arrival in 1876 were nothing short of astonishing. What had once been a simple, undeveloped agrarian land had transformed itself into a continental industrial giant and a formidable military power — all within twenty-five years. For those living in America during the late 1800s, these futuristic innovations made their society feel advanced compared to the rest of the world. As new high-rise buildings transformed urban landscapes, marvels such as the railroad, the telegram and the telephone together provided faster communication and travel, thereby cutting wait times for everything. Both America and the entire world seemed to be shrinking.

But for Jakob, now forty-three, the period between 1894 and 1900 became a time of rest. Having been married for a year and a half, he still had mixed feelings about the woman he had lost. Nevertheless, he also knew it to be one of the happiest periods of his adult life. Now retired and no longer a bachelor, a bright future lay ahead. To celebrate his retirement and as a belated honeymoon, he and his wife went on a well-deserved trip to Europe.

On Tuesday, July 10, 1894, a mere five days after Jakob's long-held business, Schleicher, Schumm & Company was renamed The Otto Gas Engine Works, he and his wife boarded a ship bound for Antwerp, Belgium. This trip back to Europe was both a refreshing vacation and an opportunity for Jakob and Elvina to enjoy each other's company, reminisce and once again see the old country. The couple stayed in Europe for four months, not returning home until mid-November. During this trip they also visited Elvina's hometown of Hannover, Germany, which was less than 300 miles from Antwerp.

Jakob had lived in America for almost twenty years, Elvina even longer, so there was much catching up for them to do. Three of Jakob's siblings (including Adolph) had passed away during this two-decade span. Of the ten Schleicher children, only five now remained. Elvina's heart was warmed as she reunited with family and friends. But like Jakob, she also counted many loved ones' births and deaths that had occurred over her long absence.

Upon completion of their trip, a renewed Jakob and Elvina Schleicher returned to Philadelphia with new roles and duties. No longer operating a business, Jakob quietly began to enjoy his retirement. For Elvina, having a retired, stay-at-home husband was a change of pace. No longer at liberty to shop, entertain or freely call on friends for tea like before, she adjusted to spending more time with her mate.

When the opportunity presented itself in early 1895 for Jakob to write about his experience on the birth and commercial development of the gas engine in America, he warmly accepted the offer. The opportunity to craft such a piece gave Jakob time to spend on one of his favorite hobbies—writing. As Jakob began writing the article for the periodical *Gas Age*, he savored the chance to evaluate the history of the gas engine, and drew liberally from his eighteen years of personal experience in the industry. If nothing else, writing this article gave him something to do; he still had not fully adjusted to having so much free time on his hands.

Beginning with the May 1, 1895 issue, and continuing for the next three issues, Jakob's personal account appeared in *Gas Age*.

"The paper of Mr. James Schleicher will doubtlessly be found of exceptional interest to all our readers," begins the editor's introduction to the series of articles. Readers are further assured that "Mr. Schleicher no longer has the slightest business connection with those handling the Otto Engine [thus,] the complete impartiality and the reliance placed upon his statements as history which could come as fitly from no other pen."

As the Schleicher & Schumm Engine Factory was a well-established and recognized manufacturer during the 1880s and early 1890s, Jakob's retirement in 1894 was widely documented in local newspapers, as well as in regional engine and gas periodicals. Many people no doubt wondered why a man of his business stature would suddenly retire. While Jakob went to great lengths in his 1895 article to educate readers about the early pioneers of the engine industry and the various challenges he faced, he failed to address the real reason why he retired. Although technology was changing, threatening the future of anyone whose livelihood depended on engine production, there was a deeper reason underlying his decision. Quite simply, Jakob was tired. The numerous losses he had recently suffered, including the passing of his brother, Adolph, had taken their toll.

In what was likely America's first behind-the-scenes look at the early gas engine industry, readers of *Gas Age* followed along as Jakob mixed his love of engineering and a passion for writing in this series of articles.

While it satisfied Jakob deeply to have been able to share his firsthand knowledge and history of gas engines, in his memoir he curiously left out any information about how his article was received by its readers. Interestingly, however, portions of his serialized article from *Gas Age* were later quoted in other periodicals, keeping alive through roughly the end of the decade

JAKOB'S STORY AND THE AMERICAN DREAM

Jakob's immigrant story and the story of the Otto Four Stroke Engine in America.

There remains little doubt that during his retirement Jakob and his wife enjoyed quite a comfortable life. To some, Jakob and Elvina's lifestyle — complete with a live-in housemaid — seemed very cosmopolitan. At the time, they lived in a three-level, red brick house on North Nineteenth Street in the affluent area of Philadelphia just south of Logan Square. By the late 1890s, when wealth was measured by whether one had electricity and indoor plumbing in their home, by the clothing one wore, and by home ownership, Jakob and his wife were traveling to Europe and frequenting their three properties in Philadelphia, Atlantic City and Pueblo, Colorado. By these standards one can conclude that Jakob and his wife were part of America's upper class.

As the Gilded Age was coming to a close, so too was the Victorian Era. Named after Queen Victoria, America's Victorian Era mimicked the high society of the British. The Queen's influence in American society could be seen in an assortment of mainstream trends. These included the way Americans dressed, their mannerisms and their favored architecture styles. Jakob, too, was influenced by these trends. Like all gentlemen seen in public during this period, he regularly sported a three-piece suit consisting of trousers, a waistcoat (vest), and tailcoat. Mandatory accessories included a wing-tipped collar shirt, a loosely knotted necktie, a hat — and of particular note — a pocket watch. With facial hair also in style, Jakob's brown and gray mustache and Van Dyke beard were trademarks he sported throughout this period.

Like the British elite, Jakob deeply valued history, his heritage, as well as his family lineage. He was proud to be able to recite his widespread ancestral line. Jakob came from a long line of German public servants, military generals, and African explorers. He and Elvina exacted correct behavior from others, but held themselves to even higher standards, befitting their class. They strove on every occasion to fulfill their social responsibility. Lewis Mumford recounts one episode at his aunt and uncle's home when a pauper came to their door. "Though chary of money handouts, Aunt Elvina would prepare sandwiches for poor hungry men with the same care that she would for members of her family, only cutting the bread a little thicker; and in winter would sometimes come back from the door with tears of pity in her eyes." While Jakob and Elvina's social etiquette may have been influenced by the moral views of the period, Jakob Schleicher was nonetheless a multifaceted and complex man. For all his devotion to engineering and finance, Jakob was a delicate man, once described by this same nephew as having "the hands of an artist and the soul of a poet."

Sitting at his desk, Jakob reached into his pants pocket and retrieved his pocket watch. It read 3:00 PM. As he looked at the watch, he thought of much more than just the time. This watch was given to him as a wedding gift by his late wife and Jakob had grown accustomed to carrying it everywhere he went. The attachment to this watch, while sentimental, was also telling. It represented the value Jakob put on time. "There is no second to be lost or wasted," Jakob regularly recited. In fact, this was yet another experience Jakob observed that took place during the Gilded Age—time standardization. This watch also reminded him of a conversation he once had with Lewis about time and always being "on the clock."

"The clock, not the engine, is the key machine of the industrial age," Lewis Mumford claimed. "The more finely we divided and measured time, first into hours, then minutes and seconds, the less we seem to have of it and the more the clock encroached upon and usurped sovereignty over life, until today we are all 'on the clock,'" Mumford believed. While Jakob disputed this point, it did ring true. As a businessman, Jakob realized that time was money, but he proudly and stubbornly defended his stance on the relative importance of his built product over incorporeal concepts such as time.

In addition to traveling with his wife, Jakob spent much of his retirement enjoying his hobbies such as reading poetry, writing and tending to his rose garden. Without any children of his own, Jakob also began spending increased amounts of time with his stepson, Adolph. Whether it was going to the beach, the pier, or playing chess at home, Jakob embraced Adolph as his own.

Jakob was forty-nine years old when the twentieth century began. He recounted this period as being a time of hope and of new beginnings. As a memento to mark the turn of the century, Jakob had saved the December 31, 1899 issue of *The New York Times* newspaper. From his desk, he walked over to his file cabinet and retrieved the old newspaper from one of the drawers. Glossing over its contents, he noticed the copious amount of real estate that had been devoted to the reviewing of various events from the nineteenth century. "We step upon the threshold of 1900 which leads to the new century, facing a still brighter dawn of civilization," the newspaper editor had noted. Reflecting back, Jakob could recount the feeling of hope and promise as the twentieth century began.

Americans in 1900 felt a sense of promise but also a sense of responsibility as a popular author of the period, Walter Lord explained. "The arrival of a new era is felt and not measured."

The start of the twentieth century in America picked up where the nineteenth had left off, with big business expanding. Although farming remained the largest industry in America, a definite shift was taking place. By 1900 America's urban population had increased eighty-seven times over. Three cities in America now had a population over one million: New York, Chicago and Jakob's home city of twenty-four years, Philadelphia. As most cities began expanding, surrounding suburbs were also in development. Urbanization brought about new forms of transportation to shuttle the masses, such as streetcars and subway systems. "We stand on the threshold of a new century big with the fate of mighty nations. It rests with us now to decide whether in the opening years of that century we shall march forward to fresh triumphs or whether at the outset we shall cripple ourselves," a politician by the name of Theodore Roosevelt stated later that year at the 1900 Republican National Convention. It seemed that America had collectively heard Mr. Roosevelt's cry, because this same period also saw the birth of another revolutionary form of transportation — air travel.

On December 17, 1903 brothers Orville and Wilbur Wright successfully launched and sustained air travel in their flying machine. Although the Wright Brothers were not the first to build a plane or attempt flight, their imaginative concept succeeded and fell in line with the hopes and dreams all Americans had at the start of the twentieth century. Across America there was no mistaking the feeling of prosperity, as well as a sense of optimism and confidence. America had once again proved it was the land where anything was possible.

As technology brought about social advancement, likewise hopes of prosperity brought immigrants to America in droves. Steadily increasing since the end of the Civil War, by 1907 im-

JAKOB'S STORY AND THE AMERICAN DREAM

migration to America peaked when 1.3 million people from around the world made the United States their new home.

As Stephan Briganti, president and CEO of the Statue of Liberty-Ellis Island Foundation, explains it, "A number of famines in Europe, the pogroms in Eastern Europe and in Russia just happen to coincide with the industrializing of America. The need in America was great and the desire to move from places that people were living in Europe and the Middle East was also substantial, so they came here."

By the start of the twentieth century, big business had catapulted the United States to the top of the list of wealthiest countries in the world. Much of the credit for this progress was a result of the presence of these same immigrants, who comprised fifty percent of America's workforce. Additionally, American business was expanding to new markets in China and other areas of Asia. With its many natural resources such as coal, wheat, sugar and cotton, America became the envy of the world. Soon, the modernization of America would have an impact on Jakob Schleicher. As it turned out, his retirement was rather short-lived.

Having been retired for five and a half years, Jakob, like many other Americans, had a bold plan and could hardly wait to try it out. In 1900 he was ready to try his hand at owning and operating a new business.

CHAPTER 11

The Philadelphia Caramel Company

We make but one thing and we make that well.
We make CARAMELS and we make the BEST in the market.
—**Philadelphia Caramel Company's slogan from 1902 advertisement**

Toward the end of the nineteenth century, America was in a severe economic depression. However, from 1897 to 1900 President William McKinley led the country through a slow recovery. President McKinley gained support from his economic plan after his decisive victory in the Spanish-American War of 1898. On a personal level, President McKinley's greatest strength was his ability to interact with ordinary people. Whether it was providing a warm smile, a pat on the shoulder, or giving an encouraging word in his soft tone, this former Civil War hero enjoyed every opportunity to interact with the public as much as his schedule permitted. His trademark phrase "Glad to see you," and his fast, mechanical handshake were always well-received.

Thanks to his military victories and his warm personality, William McKinley won a second presidential term in November of 1900. It would also be his close engagement with the public that ultimately cost him his life. On September 6, 1901 at a public engagement, having rejected the security measures available to him, McKinley was assassinated by Polish American anarchist, Leon Czolgosz. Eight days after being shot, America's twenty-fifth president died at the age of fifty-eight. On September 13 Vice President Theodore Roosevelt, who had famously been climbing Mount Marcy, was summoned back to Washington and soberly sworn in as the new president. "It shall be my aim to continue absolutely unbroken the policy of President McKinley for the peace and prosperity and honor of our beloved country," Roosevelt declared.

While the circumstances that brought Teddy Roosevelt into power were tragic, the timing could not have been more ideal. Roosevelt, nicknamed the "Buffalo Express," had progressive ideas tied directly to the advancements that were taking place in America. Seeking to keep society up with the changes technology had wrought, Roosevelt looked to eliminate corruption within the government while also reining in big business. A beacon of hope for the average citizen, Roosevelt's famous saying, "Believe and you are halfway there," set a positive tone for America's burgeoning national spirit of inventiveness. With the strong work ethic and bright outlook most Americans already possessed, along with the creativity and optimism which was being infused into society, and now with Teddy Roosevelt's encouraging support, inventors surfaced all across the forty-five United States. George Eastman's Brownie camera, the flashlight, Henry Ford's Model A automobile, and the Wright Brothers' flying machine all emerged during this era. These inventions were amazing; they in turn brought about an easier and more improved way of life for Americans.

Typing in his office that morning, Jakob recounted all of these events. He also remembered how one other event from February 1900 changed his future. While some had read about it, others, like Jakob, had heard about it. There was an unmistakable chatter going around town. A fellow Philadelphian had just produced America's first chocolate bar. This same man had been in the news a couple of years prior, when he sold his Lancaster Caramel candy factory for an unprecedented one million dollars. He had now reinvented himself and was producing edible chocolate treats. His name was Milton Hershey.

Although chocolate had been around for many years, by 1900 it was still considered an expensive specialty. Prior to 1900, chocolate could only be purchased by American consumers in the form of a coating over a piece of fruit or covering a small piece of sweet candy. While the thought of creating an entire chocolate bar was dismissed as being simply too expensive, the production of Hershey's chocolate bars piqued Jakob's interest. Although he had been happily retired for a little more than five years, he had started feeling a bit restless.

Jakob was neither a gambler nor an overly prudent individual, but as with his initial venture to America he believed that, in order to find success, some degree of risk was necessary. "Being a capitalist by conviction as well as by acquisition, Uncle Jakob felt morally obliged to invest his fortune, not in safe rentier's securities, but in enterprises involving risk," stated Lewis Mumford. Just as he and his wife felt a sense of social responsibility, Jakob also felt an obligation to expend some of his net worth for the potential of a greater return. He decided to start his own candy business.

Also prompting his new venture was the magic he recalled feeling on that special Easter morning of his youth when he discovered the candy and eggs that were left for him. While manufacturing candy became a means of creating happiness for everyone who consumed his product, it also was a way for Jakob to find fulfillment. Whereas Jakob indeed found companionship in his marriage, this relationship lacked the depth of intimacy, passion and contentment he was looking for. Therefore, operating a candy business would be about more than just manufacturing and selling sweets. In a very real sense, this endeavor took the place of what was lacking in his marriage and became his passion for the next fifteen years. In this manner, Jakob's reward was in the journey itself. The time was right, Jakob felt, to try his hand at candy making.

On May 15, 1900, with firmness of purpose and more than a little excitement, Jakob Schleicher invested $25,000 to begin his new business venture. He selected Philadelphia Caramel Company as the name of his business. By 1900 the term *Philadelphia caramel* had become a popular catch phrase to describe a chewy morsel of chocolate caramel. Several confectioners made their own versions, along with various other formulations that included strawberry, coffee and vanilla. Though he didn't note a reason in his memoir, Jakob may have adopted his company name to capitalize on consumers' already-established associations.

Another explanation could be that as a longtime Philadelphia resident, Jakob chose his company's name as an act of pride in "his" city and as an easily recognizable geographical location where his business was located. Regardless, with a name selected and his business newly incorporated, Jakob continued preparations.

As with the engine business he had previously operated, Jakob was in need of a business partner. His choice was simple and nonpareil. He selected his stepson, Adolph Ebeling. By this time, Adolph Ebeling was a mature thirty year-old. Having watched him grow through the years, Jakob not only knew his stepson's character and trustworthiness, but he was also familiar with Adolph's work ethic from when they worked together at the Schleicher & Schumm factory. This selection had a deeper, more significant meaning, too. Through this one act Jakob embraced Adolph as his own son. Feeling confident in his selection, Jakob assigned Adolph the positions of vice president and treasurer of the company.

Father and son business partners, Jakob and Adolph quickly located a suitable factory for their business in northern Philadelphia. Sandwiched between nearby landmarks Penn Treaty Park and the Shackamaxon Street Ferry, and located in an industrial area known as Fishtown, this readily accessible facility had ports and railroad systems for the transportation of employees, goods and supplies. There was also a sugar refinery nearby. It was the ideal location.

In their final stage of preparation, Jakob and Adolph began the long, arduous task of seeking and hiring workers. Men, women and children ages thirteen and up were interviewed to fill various positions such as wrappers, icers, chocolate coaters, caramel and nougat slicers, candy rollers, errand runners and machinists. Women and children were hired to work some of the less demanding assignments while men were employed to take on the more rigorous tasks at the factory.

As was typical during this period, wages were not standardized. Thus, as a nonunion factory and with a lack of organization amongst its workers, pay rates varied widely. In general, men working the more dangerous and physically demanding positions made more money than women. Women with prior experience in the candy field earned more than those new to the trade, or those who were assigned to wrapping and boxing. Meanwhile, children were tasked mostly with errands such as fetching and carrying supplies to different workstations and were paid the least. While Jakob and Adolph were co-owners, it was Adolph's responsibility to hire and determine the employees' salaries. Any system Adolph devised to set salaries or pay bonuses, for example, to employees with exceptional attendance such as beginning on time and not missing work due to illness, were not Jakob's concern. In overseeing the overall financial aspect of his business, Jakob knew the average weekly salary for a candy factory employee in 1900 was about four dollars a week.

Generally, the turnover rate for workers in the candy trade circa 1900 was about fifty percent, as the average length of employment only lasted around six months. On the other hand, the same level of employment was not maintained throughout the year. "In a candy factory one is always laid off for a couple of weeks after Christmas and of course during summer," one interviewee explained. It was also during the holidays that additional helpers, such as bakers, were hired to decorate Easter eggs or similar seasonal items.

In keeping with another trend of the period, most workers at large candy plants specialized in only one assignment (making of creams, fondants, nougats, etc.). Women exclusively assigned to "chocolate dipping" duties were considered skilled laborers and were among the highest paid workers at the factory.

Jakob's Philadelphia Caramel Company did not specialize in any one confection. Instead they sold a range of products, both wholesale and retail, from their own line of penny goods to their finer line of chocolates in which each chocolate was designated a tier and title. These included Belmars, Deltas, Galatea, and their top of the line Sultanas. Some other curious candy names included Big Button Caramels, Crown Drops, and Neptunes.

By the spring of 1901 a full staff of 150 employees was on hand for production of the company's initial batch. After having built the business from scratch, Jakob couldn't wait to watch his new operation get underway. Carefully observing his workers during the first phase of the candy making process, Jakob proudly remembers exclaiming, "We make but one thing and we make that well. We make CARAMELS and we make the BEST in the market." This slogan quickly became this company's mantra and was used as a promotional slogan in their early years of advertising.

Jakob also recalled how, over the years, visitors such as state inspectors, jobbers and family members frequented the factory. He took pride in giving tours. Nephew Lewis Mumford shared his unique perspective from when he visited the plant. "It amazed me to find, when I went through the candy factory with Cousin Adolph, what familiar human terms he was with his workers, calling them [each] by their first names," he wrote. Others who visited the factory were able to witness firsthand the process of raw materials being transformed into a wide variety of goods and treats.

As he reflected on his years of producing candy, Jakob relaxed. It was a pleasant and familiar subject. He had always been proud of his days as a confectioner and felt this occupation defined him. Although he was never considered an innovator in the candy field, Jakob did well for himself as sales averaged between $100,000 and $150,000 annually.

Located just to the east of Philadelphia, along the bank of the Delaware River, is the state of New Jersey and the city of Camden. Incorporated in 1828, Camden's most popular citizen, Walt Whitman, once compared this city to other cities he previously resided in. "Camden was originally an accident—but I shall never be sorry. I was left over in Camden. It has brought me blessed returns." Over the years the city of Camden brought blessing and returns to its other citizens and businesses as well.

The city of Camden had been experiencing unprecedented growth during America's industrialization period of the late nineteenth and early twentieth centuries. Between the years 1870 and 1920 Camden's population had increased nearly six times over, exploding from a mere 20,000 in 1870 to 116,000 in 1920. "Camden 1900–1910 was growing by leaps and bounds," city historian Phil Cohen explained. City government focused almost exclusively on business development, expanding the transportation system to include ferries, rail, and trolley routes. "Camden was THE place to go if you had an idea and wanted to make money," Cohen added.

With a number of big name manufacturers such as Campbell's Soup Factory, the Victor Talking Machine Company (later RCA Victor), and the New York Shipbuilding Company already having planted roots in Camden, this city seemed to be a sensible and ideal location for Jakob and Adolph to relocate their thriving candy business. After four years in operation, Jakob and Adolph's confectionery business was flourishing. Philadelphia Caramel Company's volume of output actually became problematic, as its facilities were now inadequate to store the thousands of pounds of candy produced daily. Jakob noted in his memoir that while his company was outgrowing their Beach Street factory, both production and profits exceeded even his original expectations. The search for a location that would facilitate their growth began in early 1905.

Prices of Camden properties were on the rise, but when an available riverfront lot became available for purchase, Jakob proceeded to acquire it, building a new facility and finally relocating the Philadelphia Caramel Company across the Delaware River. A large 260- by 180-foot modern candy manufacturing plant was erected on the site at the cost of $65,000. It was in close proximity to nearby railroads, steamship wharves, sugar refineries and ferries. Giving employment to an additional 100 persons and bringing the company's total number of employees to 250, Jakob's candy company changed its name to Philadelphia Caramel Company of Camden, New Jersey. His new two-story factory opened its doors for business in July, 1905 — a mere five months after locating and purchasing the property.

As savvy American consumers continued looking for the newest, most creative confectionery treats and with competition from a number of other brands, Jakob was pleased to find himself earning a larger share in the candy market. Toward the end of his first decade in the candy trade, Jakob had successfully leveraged his business skills of goal setting, innovation and passion to take the Philadelphia Caramel Company to the next level. These were no doubt becoming the golden years of the Philadelphia Caramel Company, but two upcoming battles were rapidly approaching.

CHAPTER 12

The Three Uninvited Guests

Three things come into the house uninvited:
debts, age and death.
— **German Proverb**

Two weeks had passed since Jakob's last doctor visit. Upon returning to Jakob's home for a recheck, the doctor became concerned. Jakob's condition was not improving. In fact, his minor cold had worsened. Jakob was now displaying symptoms of dehydration. It was a combination of the listlessness, the shallow breathing and the glassy eyes that worried the doctor. In addition, Jakob also explained to his physician that over the past few days he was finding it more difficult to simply get around the house as he was becoming winded rather rapidly. Menial tasks, such as walking from one room to the next, or preparing a meal, were becoming more of a challenge. With this sudden deterioration in his health, Jakob feared having a medical emergency, and it was possible no one would be home to help him. He had declined to ask his family for assistance in the past, impressing on them that his health was not their responsibility.

Considering the situation for a moment the doctor told Jakob to make himself comfortable on his bed. The doctor decided the best form of rehydration treatment was to administer an IV. As he started to monitor his patient and was pulling up a nearby chair, Jakob spontaneously recited the following German poem: "Three things come into the house uninvited: debts, age and death." More and more, Jakob felt, this poem rang true. After a brief pause the doctor admitted that at age seventy-four, death was indeed catching up to Jakob, but the doctor promised he would do his best to slow down the process as much as possible.

In late 1908 Jakob first began to take note of these uninvited guests. He had occasion that year to ponder his age. At the time Jakob was fifty-seven years old and his wife was sixty-six. Life expectancy at the time was age fifty, but up to that point their ages hadn't meant much. In August that year Jakob received word from Europe that his youngest sister, Clara, had passed away at the youthful age of forty-seven. The loss of his sister drove Jakob to think about his own mortality. Losing his baby sister, who was still so young, so vibrant and full of life brought home this realization—age and death did not necessarily work in conjunction. From that point on, Jakob wisely used his sister's death as a reminder that every day was a gift and that he should probably take steps to prepare for his and his wife's final years.

Soon after Clara's death, Jakob and Elvina decided that at their age they could stand to downsize from their three-level home. Having resided in Philadelphia for over thirty years, Jakob and Elvina moved into a newly built Dutch Colonial home in the upper-middle-class neighborhood of Merchantville, New Jersey. This move out of the big city and into a smaller suburb was going to be a change of pace for both of them, but at this point in their lives it was exactly what they were looking for. This move also provided Jakob the additional benefit of having a closer commute to his candy factory located in the neighboring city of Camden.

Then, just a few years later, one of Jakob's younger brothers, Wilfred, also passed away unexpectedly; he was fifty-four. From his once large family of ten children, now only three remained: an older sister, a younger brother and Jakob. Age and death were no longer off in a distance. In a very real sense they not only seemed to be closing in, but were doing so at a rapid pace. To further bring home this point, only weeks after Wilfred's death Elvina and Jakob both celebrated birthdays. She turned seventy and he turned sixty-one. A month later they soberly celebrated their twentieth wedding anniversary.

Following their wedding anniversary that December, Elvina's health began changing. At first she became irritable and unusually tired. Jakob sensed something was amiss, but to keep harmony in the home he quietly brushed aside her odd behavior. Elvina on the other hand, unknowingly dismissed these symptoms as just part of getting older. She initially avoided telling her husband of these sudden changes, as she did not think it was that serious an issue. But after a few weeks of not feeling her normal self, she reluctantly decided to inform her husband.

After Elvina shared her health issue with her husband, certain things began to make sense. Jakob had noticed a slight change in his wife's character; her usual passion for cleanliness had become an obsession. Elvina was also becoming noticeably upset at relatively minor issues. The household had also gone through an unusually high number of maids. Along with this peculiar behavior, Elvina's bouts with fatigue were becoming much more noticeable. Lewis Mumford, the couple's nephew, recalled going to visit them on Christmas, 1912. "We found her in tears, either because another maid had just left or because the lace curtains she had just put up clean a few days before were already blackened." At that point Jakob realized her behavior must be due to ill health. They agreed to see their family doctor.

As the fluid continued to pump into his arm while still lying on his bed, Jakob thought back to 1913 and recounted the trial he was about to go through back then. He shared with his doctor the details of that cold January day when it all began. It was a Monday. Upon arriving at the doctor's office that morning, Elvina went through a battery of tests. With some minor level of anxiety they waited for the results to come back from the lab. A week later they returned to the doctor's office where they received a diagnosis: Elvina had cancer — specifically breast cancer. Although the medical field had made moderate advancements by 1900, a cancer diagnosis in 1913 was still considered a death sentence. Elvina's doctor explained there was little that could be done to help her. This news caught the couple completely off guard. Having difficulty processing this information, they simply held each other's hands in the doctor's office and wept together. For several days after this doctor visit the tears continued. Both were fully aware that Elvina's life would be coming to a painful close.

In 1913 breast cancer was poorly understood. At the time there was much debate in the medical field over whether breast cancer was an infectious disease. Treatment was also disputed. Dr. James Syme, an early pioneer surgeon and president of the Royal College of Surgeons of Edinburgh, Scotland, understood cancer well enough to know the only effective procedure for defeating this deadly disease was to remove it completely. However, it was also Dr. Syme's opinion that breast cancer surgery should not be attempted as "it would be subjecting the patient to useless pain and could bring surgery into discredit to attempt extirpation in cases where the extent of connections of the diseases prevented its complete removal." For those patients who had the money and elected to have a mastectomy, the results were uniformly unfavorable: they died shortly after surgery as a result of sepsis, an infection of the blood, as sterilizing of medical tools was not yet widely practiced.

Although Jakob and Elvina could have afforded the surgery, they elected not to proceed. They felt it would, in essence, hasten death. Throughout 1913 Elvina's health slowly deteriorated. As the cancer grew, Elvina's strength weakened and the couple stopped traveling. Eventually even going to church became such a difficult task that their minister regularly came to their home to pray and provide much-needed spiritual and emotional support to both of them. Meanwhile, Jakob and Adolph's candy business suffered dramatically. Both men were frequently absent from the factory and office, instead spending their time caring for and tending to Elvina. It was also during his wife's illness that Jakob began to realize how meaningful she was to him. As he focused his attention on his dying wife, the depth of their relationship that had been lacking flourished as they spent their last several months' together.

While still lying down, Jakob once again thought about the uninvited guests from the German poem. In great detail, the pain from this one period in his life returned. Jakob also briefly recalled how, throughout the time he was tending to Elvina, he would often quietly slip away into another room and weep over how the cancer was sapping her life away. Tending to a terminally ill patient not only proved to be an emotional rollercoaster, but it was also mentally draining and physically demanding. Even for someone in Elvina's social class, palliative care was minimal. It consisted of having a private nurse stop at their home several times a week to check in and tend to the patient. While such care improved the quality of life for this family to some degree, ultimately it could not take away Jakob's grief or sadness. Finally, on the morning of Thursday, March 5, 1914 Elvina Schleicher passed away. Thanks in large part to a fellow Philadelphian, Anna Jarvis, it was nine weeks after Elvina's death that Jakob was given the opportunity to honor his late wife in a very special way.

Anna Jarvis was an outspoken activist in her community. Additionally, she was very active in the church she attended: Andrews Methodist Episcopal Church. In 1876 Anna began praying for a national day to commemorate mothers. "I hope and pray that someone, sometime, will found a memorial mother's day commemorating her for the matchless service she renders to humanity in every field of life. She is entitled to it," Jarvis once remarked. Jarvis later broadened the concept to recognize all mothers, living and dead, and continued her campaign for three decades. Gradually her movement gained popularity and momentum. It finally reached President Woodrow Wilson at the White House in the spring of 1914. On May 9, 1914 the President signed into law a new holiday — Mother's Day — to be celebrated every second Sunday in the month of May. Since her mother's favorite flowers were carnations, Anna Jarvis arranged that everyone in her church would wear a carnation on the first Mother's Day in 1914. Red carnations were to be worn for mothers who were alive, while white carnations were worn to remember each mother who had died.

JAKOB'S STORY AND THE AMERICAN DREAM

On Sunday, May 10, 1914 Jakob proudly attended church wearing a white carnation in remembrance of his late wife and his own mother, who had been gone for over a decade.

As the doctor disconnected the IV, he noticed that Jakob had gotten some color back and seemed to have a bit more energy. Pleased, the doctor put his equipment away. He ordered his patient to increase his fluid intake and get extra rest. He would visit again in forty-eight hours but would be continuously available if an emergency arose. Agreeing to these terms, Jakob showed his doctor to the door.

Feeling better, Jakob returned to working on his memoirs. Knowing exactly where to resume, he once again made his way over to his library and began typing. All that he had just recounted over the past hour while lying on the couch brought back the emptiness he had been feeling for the past twelve years since his wife's passing. Writing helped him fill the emptiness. Compassion for Elvina, who had lost her first husband in 1889, flowed in to fill the void.

Next came a few drops of resentment. Being alone after his wife's death was difficult. Having cut back the budget for in-home help, Jakob took over the cooking and housework. He attended family get-togethers and social gatherings alone. Whenever he did attend these types of events he would frequently be asked how he was doing, or what life was like without Elvina. He politely responded, but quietly he seethed over these questions. If he were to answer honestly, he'd have to describe how, within the first year of her death there were many days and nights when he simply cried uncontrollably — but mentioning this would surely make others uncomfortable. As the days turned into weeks, and the weeks into months, the mourning gradually subsided, but the emptiness never completely went away.

Jakob also thought back to 1881 and Elvina Baron. He reasoned that if he had chosen to pursue the younger Elvina Baron over her aunt, the widow Elvina Ebeling, he might have been spared the pain of losing a wife. A year after his wife's passing Jakob sought to reestablish a relationship with Elvina Baron.

"In that period Uncle Jakob's renewed love for my mother, now openly declared, led him to write…long letters and tender poems to my mother," Lewis Mumford explained. However, much had taken place in the thirty-four years since their abrupt break up in 1881. Jakob had changed. Elvina Baron had changed. In fact, the entire world had changed. But there was one thing that had not changed: Elvina Baron's sense of betrayal.

Elvina Baron wondered how could Jakob have so easily married another woman, especially after he first expressed his love for her. Granted, her aunt had become a widow, but didn't Jakob's affection and hopes of a future outweigh his responsibility to care for a widowed woman? After all, Elvina Ebeling had a son who could take care of her.

Elvina Baron summarized her feelings toward Jakob when she penned a brief entry into her diary in 1924:

> A life wasted but for one redeeming feature. To wake up one day and realize life has passed you by without the dreams, hopes and longings fulfilled, is a thing words cannot tell the meaning of, living always in the thought that a change would come and the ambitions of a lifetime come to pass, to live and feel the bitterness of what might have been.

With this letter "My mother's secret was bared," Mumford remembered. "Had my mother married [the man] she loved, she would probably have been capable of giving a full measure of happiness and of being deeply fulfilled, with a family of many children instead of a single one," Mumford insightfully explained. "Aunt Elvina wrecked three lives; for she bore Uncle Jakob no child of his own and if my mother and Uncle Jakob both paid for the separation (of 1881), so did she," Mumford added.

In regard to his uncle, Lewis Mumford believed the loss of his wife was just the tip of the iceberg. More changes were afoot in the 1910s, changes that would affect Jakob, his candy business and millions around the globe. By the end of the decade the world would be forever changed.

CHAPTER 13

The Great War

Victory will come to the side that outlasts the other.
—**Ferdinand Foch, French General, Western Front**

Distraught over the loss of his companion, Jakob gradually withdrew from social life. He and Elvina had shared twenty plus years of simple moments together. While their marriage was to some degree a union of convenience, there was nonetheless a level of comfort in each other's company, as well as a long-term friendship, which was now lost. Losing all of this was simply overwhelming. Immediately following Elvina's death in March 1914, Jakob delegated the most crucial business decisions to his stepson, Adolph. Adolph too was subdued over his mother's death, but unlike Jakob, Adolph was able to go home to his wife and children, who provided him the emotional support he needed to get through this difficult time.

After being home for nearly a month, Jakob forced himself to return to work simply as an effort to take his mind off the loss of his wife. Although he tried desperately to refocus his efforts and attention into his candy business, something clearly had changed. Jakob not only had to adjust to being alone in their empty home and living by himself, but his overall outlook, his compassion and his sympathy toward others had numbed.

Unable to cope with the silence, Jakob soon moved out of his home and once again began renting a room just so he wouldn't have to live alone. Then, as if his world hadn't been turned upside down enough, a mere 145 days after Elvina's passing another event shook Jakob—and the entire European continent. The tension that had been building between Germany and its neighbors finally erupted into a large-scale war.

The tension in Europe stemmed from imperialism, or the policy of one country extending their influence over another country. In the early twentieth century America was no stranger to imperialism. Under the leadership of President Theodore Roosevelt, the United States imposed an aggressive foreign policy on Central America and Panama. In addition, American influence could be felt as far away as the Philippines as America took control of these islands. In Europe, the "Scramble for Africa" saw colonizer countries such as Britain, France and Germany invade and occupy territories in Africa looking for gold and diamonds. While Britain and France occupied large overseas empires, Germany resented that they occupied a much smaller percentage of territory. This issue was becoming more and more a source of contention between Germany and its powerful rivals, but there were other political issues festering too.

The German government felt strongly that their country deserved a larger role in international affairs, just as they had back in the nineteenth century during Otto von Bismarck's rule (1862–1890). As early as New Year's Day 1900, Germany's emperor, Kaiser Wilhelm had envisioned the return of Germany to her "place in the sun." To achieve this, the kaiser started Germany on a new course. Hoping to increase Germany's influence in Europe and abroad, the kaiser focused on building Germany's naval fleet. In response, the British and the Russians began strengthening their own militaries. By 1914 Germany had become a formidable power in the region, but feeling surrounded by hostile neighbors, was driven into isolation.

As Germany, Britain and other countries in the region were strengthening their militaries, simultaneously smaller Slavic states such as Serbia, Bosnia, Croatia and Slovakia were collectively seeking independence from Austria-Hungary. Military historian Richard Holmes described the events leading up to the First World War as a calamity that no one was able to control.

"Political and military leaders were wrestling with problems quite beyond their resources," Holmes explained. One of these political leaders was America's president, Woodrow Wilson. Wilson attempted to deescalate the growing tension in the region, but as these countries inched closer to conflict, many throughout Europe felt war was inevitable. As the impending feeling of war filled the air, pep rally-type events began sweeping across Germany. These flag-waving processions were intended to inspire German patriotism and eventually became known as the Spirit of 1914. At the same time many Europeans began hoarding food in preparation for war. Suddenly, on June 28, 1914 one key event took place that virtually assured the start of war. As a statement to show their dedication to ending the Austro-Hungarian occupation in Bosnia-Herzegovina, Serbian nationalist Gavrilo Princip assassinated Kaiser Wilhelm's close friend and heir to the Austrian throne, Archduke Franz Ferdinand.

Having always been proud of his German heritage, Jakob had never given voice publicly to his political views before the start of the European War. But after the death of his wife, Jakob needed something else to focus on. He became increasingly preoccupied with Germany and the political crises of the period. "[As] the First World War came on, like so many Germans in America, he (Uncle Jakob) was more imperial than Kaiser," Lewis Mumford remembered. Mirroring many of the same beliefs as the kaiser, Jakob took a strong disliking toward the British. While neither the kaiser nor Jakob acknowledged Germany's imperialistic ambitions, they were both quick to point out their distain toward Britain and, as they saw it, British imperialism.

The kaiser's animosity toward the British was personal. As a result of an accident at birth, young Wilhelm's left arm was deformed and was rendered useless. He blamed his mother's doctor, who was of British descent, for the inability to repair or to make use of the arm. In a similar way, Jakob took Britain's insults to his beloved poetry personally. "[Uncle Jakob] viewed all of England's traditions with cold contempt, down to the fact that these barbarians degraded the sacred classics by calling (authors) Titus Livius 'Livy' and Marcus Tullius Cicero 'Tully,'" Lewis recounted. At first Jakob's distain for the British seemed somewhat peculiar. After all, he had heretofore embraced Victorian fashion, values, mannerisms and morality. But Jakob's unwavering loyalty was now clearly with Germany.

Having amassed large amounts of weaponry, each country's official line was that they would quickly devastate their enemy. Such a war "would be over before the leaves finished falling," University of California-Berkeley professor J. Bradford DeLong explained. However, many indications pointed to an extended "people's war" with massive casualties. In 1890 Germany's retiring chief general, Helmuth von Moltke, warned of a large war lasting for years. Ivan Bloch, a Polish banker, saw on the horizon a war featuring trench combat, a high mortality rate and a devastating blow to the European economy.

On July 27, 1914 the night before war broke out, British foreign secretary Edward Grey had an inclination the world was about to change. "The lights are going out all over Europe. I do not think we shall see them lit again in our lifetime," he grimly predicted. The next day—July 28, 1914—exactly one month after Franz Ferdinand's assassination, Austria-Hungary declared war on Serbia. In a matter of days, alliances were formed that pitted the Allies against Germany and the Central Powers.

Most people could never have imagined the type of war that was about to be unleashed upon them. With advancements in technology making their way onto the battlefield, the Great War introduced the world to weapons such as tanks, aircraft, automatic machine guns and flame throwers, all of which contributed to death on a scale never before seen in the history of mankind. The days of fighting an enemy on horseback, or in hand to hand combat as in the Battle of Waterloo, had given way to aircraft bombings and machine guns capable of spitting out 400-600 rounds per minute. As a result of these weapons, tactics and strategies on the battlefield changed forever. With this overwhelming machinery, the individual soldier, not unlike an insect being stepped on by a boot, seemed smaller.

Each country involved in the war had various opportunities at stake. Germany sought to expand their empire and influence in the region. As a means to restore French predominance in Europe and to gain back Alsace and Lorraine, territories lost during the Franco-Prussian War of 1871, France had been preparing for and welcomed a war against Germany. Believing their neighbor to the east would invade them, France constructed heavy fortifications along their border with Germany. Germany went around these fortifications and invaded neutral Belgium, thereby forcing some 800,000 Belgian citizens to flee. In turn, Belgians quickly adopted the rallying cry, "We are a country, not a thoroughfare!" But Belgium's defenses were no match to Germany's massive military. Within nine short weeks of invading, Germany had taken hold of Jakob's hometown of Antwerp. Reacting to the more than 6,000 Belgian casualties, people around the world condemned Germany's acts of aggression.

Jakob meanwhile was desensitized. He dismissed Germany's actions as simply being part of war. Echoing the same sentiments as German general Friedrich von Bernardi, who described war as "a natural and positive part of human evolution" and "the great universal law which rules all life," Jakob threw all of his support into the German cause. "Unfortunately Uncle Jakob's sense of human values was sullied and betrayed by his sentimental attachment to moribund German institutions," Lewis Mumford later explained.

On September 7, 1914 — less than six weeks into the battle — the fantasy of a swift war was gone. Perceiving a long, drawn-out war was in the making, French General, Ferdinand Foch, declared, "Victory will come to the side that outlasts the other."

As this engagement entered into its first winter, the effects of an extended war became noticeable. Within the first three months of the war a total of one million soldiers had died. In addition, food, munitions and supplies on the battlefield were dwindling. Food prices around the world spiked as food became scarce. Although America was producing thirty-six percent of the world's manufactured goods, the shortages in Europe had an almost immediate effect on Jakob, as well as the rest of the United States. The war also began having a startling effect on Germans living in America.

Based simply on their ethnicity, many German immigrants in America were subjected to ridicule and hatred. Many German-Americans were forced to stay indoors and out of public view for their own safety. Fear and paranoia swept across America, as employers made employees take "loyalty oaths" to prove their patriotism. German newspapers tried to sway public opinion about the war as they published propaganda portraying the war as an attempt by the British to humble Germany and to establish British domination throughout the world. This effort accomplished little. Believing that the "European War" was far away and America was safely isolated, the United States remained neutral. However, what America initially failed to realize was how significant international trade had become and how the war was about to disrupt it.

Soon after the war broke out, "enormous orders…suddenly started to pour into America from all over the world and for all sorts of goods," the periodical, *International Confectioner*, reported. The September 1914 issue further reported that "[I]n the first week of this war, which was taking place four thousand miles away, the prices of all foodstuffs in American markets went up 50 to 100 percent in the most important commodities, and 10 to 20 percent in nearly everything else." To further exacerbate the resulting shortages, foreign governments from around the world began bidding against each other for badly needed supplies. Europe's problems had suddenly become America's business problems. While America claimed neutrality, business statistics showed otherwise. United States banks had loaned nearly ten times more money to the Allies as they did to the Central Powers.

Whereas the world's increased demand for food and other goods helped those businesses that could scale up rapidly, Jakob's Philadelphia Caramel Company was in trouble. Along with many other confectioners, Jakob had not anticipated the need to stock up on sugar. As the price of sugar spiked, purchasing this vital ingredient cut into company profits. Soaring sugar prices rapidly started to chip away at additional assets such as business and personal savings accounts. Jakob's business took on debt; he was forced to purchase raw materials on credit. "The unpleasant truth which stares the trade in the face today and will not be denied, is that a great many of our manufacturers have been forced in spite of large orders for goods, to seek extensions of time on their bills payable," the March 1916 *International Confectioner* noted. Jakob's support for the war had taken a strange twist. Instead of victory he was experiencing failure.

Eight months into the war a new weapon was unleashed on the battlefield. The date was April 15, 1915 when a strange green cloud appeared on the battlefield in Ypres, Belgium. Unannounced, the Germans deployed a gas that coincidentally took on the scent of spring. Allied soldiers were quickly incapacitated by it. The gas first affected its victim by making his eyes watery. Then, it rapidly began burning and swelling the victim's tongue. Unable to swallow or move his tongue, the affected soldier would emit a horrifying death rattle. In a matter of moments, soldiers across a wide area lay dead, becoming the first victims of mustard gas.

The use of mustard gas was simple and straightforward. The gas cloud drifted across enemy lines and attacked its victim's heart and lungs rendering an enemy soldier incapacitated. Unprotected, soldiers asphyxiated and died. For the army deploying this gas, this form of killing was generally safe as they would not have to leave their trenches. The gas would simply travel across the battlefield and decimate large numbers of enemy soldiers at once. Before the start of the war, many countries believed that the use of chemical weapons was inhumane, but even these moral objections would not stop its deployment during the war. At this juncture, German military leaders believed that the use of mustard gas would bring about a quick end to an already extended war.

Three weeks after the Germans first deployed mustard gas on the battlefield, they breached another international law by firing on a non-military ship without warning. On May 7, 1915 the *RMS Lusitania* was carrying 1,962 people aboard. It was fired upon as it was passing the south coast of Ireland. Eighteen minutes after a German U-boat fired one torpedo, the *Lusitania* sank, killing 1,198 passengers, 128 of whom were American citizens. "In God's name, how could any nation calling itself civilized do so horrible a thing?" President Woodrow Wilson asked. Equal Rights League member Samuel Schneider described the destruction of the *Lusitania* as a "colossal sin against humanity." Although Germany claimed the United States was transporting war supplies on the *Lusitania*, its sinking nonetheless put Germany in a bad light in the eyes of many Americans who had previously held a neutral stance toward Germany and the war.

Germany was well aware that a substantial German-American population existed in America. On September 8, 1915 the German embassy in the United States attempted to appeal to this faction when they urged all German citizens in America to quit working. This was an attempt to both undermine America's economy and drum up German support in America.

Philadelphia Caramel Company's Military Caramel Card, circa 1914.

British diplomats pressured President Wilson to give up his neutrality and choose which side he was going to support during the war. "There was a general anti-Europe feeling in the United States so far as being in the European War," retired United States Marine Corps Brigadier General Edwin H. Simmons explained. While America officially remained neutral, the United States was nonetheless gradually being drawn into this conflict.

For a time, Jakob remained mum on these acts of aggression by Germany. Rather than display his loyalties publicly, Jakob spoke up for the German cause among his inner circle. "Before the United States entered the war, [Uncle Jakob] used to bombard my mother and myself with pamphlets arguing the German cause," Lewis Mumford recalled. In what became his last candy company promotion, Jakob distributed military trading cards with his Philadelphia caramels. Included in each package of "Military Caramels" was a card depicting the rulers, soldiers, and flags of the six countries involved in the war. They included: Austria-Hungary, Belgium, England, France, Germany and Russia. The cards did not contain propagandistic language, but Jakob's support for Germany remained unwavering. "German literature, German ideas and ideals and many things pertaining to the practical life and methods of the Germans will command more respect and interest after the war and it is well to prepare for coming events," Jakob wrote in October 1916.

But by the end of 1916 the Central Powers were no longer optimistic about winning the war. Realizing they had reached an impasse, the German government attempted to broker a peace treaty with the Allies, under the condition that Germany be allowed to keep possession of territories they currently held. When this offer was declined, Germany quickly resumed their unrestricted naval warfare. American merchant ships were among those that were being targeted and sunk with increased regularity. This, in turn, induced a wave of anger and patriotism in America.

With the war expanding to the open seas, naval blockades by both Britain and Germany brought a new dimension to the war. These blockades prevented badly needed supplies from reaching their destinations. More importantly, however, with food supplies dangerously low on both sides, food itself was now becoming a weapon.

Realizing that the war was nearing a critical stage and that American intervention could sway the outcome, Germany devised a secret plan to distract the United States from entering the European War. The plan was for Germany's foreign minister, Arthur Zimmermann, to send the German ambassador in Mexico a diplomatic proposal for a military alliance between Germany and Mexico. The telegram, dated January 10, 1917 promised Mexico generous financial support for the purpose of "reconquering the lost territory in Texas, New Mexico and Arizona." In addition, the telegram also urged Mexico to broker an alliance with Japan. That way, America's resources would be stretched too thin to also mount a force against Germany in Europe. Before the Zimmermann Telegram, as it was called, could reach its destination, however, it was intercepted by British intelligence and handed over to American officials.

Discovering the Zimmermann Telegram was the last straw. American vessels were being targeted and sunk by German U-boats; German agents carried out attacks on American soil. Thus provoked, the United States declared war against Germany on April 6, 1917. President Woodrow Wilson provided the following explanation to the American people: "Neutrality is no longer feasible or desirable. It is a fearful thing to lead this great people into war and into the most terrible and disastrous of all wars, civilization itself seemingly being in the balance. But the right is more precious than peace. The world must be made safe for democracy."

CHAPTER 14

The Lawsuit

The heart was made to be broken.
—Oscar Wilde, author

Before he got too ahead of himself and America's entry into the European War, Jakob decided to backtrack slightly. Once again thinking about the German proverb of the uninvited guests, Jakob painfully retraced the timeline of when debt first came lurking about. He recalled how a rapid series of events took place that culminated in his financial downfall. All of these events could be tracked back to the first week of August, 1914.

Prior to the start of the Great War the three largest sugar-producing nations in the world—Germany, Austria and Russia—were producing a combined total of 7 million tons of sugar beets annually. With sugar widely available in 1913 and early 1914, its price averaged around four cents a pound. When the war began in Europe in August 1914, these three countries' priorities shifted to fighting a war and each country elected to cut back on their sugar production, thereby cutting their combined output almost in half to 4.1 million tons annually. As the war got underway, Germany suspended virtually all trading with two of its largest trade partners, Great Britain and France, almost immediately spurring dramatic and unforeseen economic problems around the world.

In September 1914 the New York-based periodical, *International Confectioner*, reported, "The sugar question is probably the most serious of all to [American] confectioners, for notwithstanding the fact that there is an enormous supply of sugar on hand, and promises of great quantities still to come, the foreign bids for vast amounts for immediate delivery forced prices away above what they should be, and there is no doubt that advantage was taken by certain sugar interests to use this as an excuse for inflation of prices....the result of this is that most of the manufacturers of candies and chocolates have been compelled to advance their prices accordingly." Consumers and businesses alike, including Jakob's Philadelphia Caramel Company, felt the pinch. Although he had weathered a few recessions during his time in America, Jakob had little to draw on to resolve this growing business crisis. Neither his classical education nor his life experience thus far held the answers.

Contributing to the sharp rise for the price of sugar in late 1914 was the shortage of German ships available to transport and distribute it. On August 8, 1914, only days into the war, Lloyd's of London reported the loss of forty-one German ships and vessels, all of which were either damaged severely or sunk in the previous twenty-four-hour period. Within the first month from the start of the war, Germany had lost twenty-five percent of her ships, either seized in harbors or caught trying to flee the country. Meanwhile, Great Britain and France quickly became dependent on the Western Hemisphere for their sugar.

JAKOB'S STORY AND THE AMERICAN DREAM

This attack on German ships was a military-style economic tactic first devised by a member of Britain's Defense Committee, Maurice Hankey. Hankey believed the only successful means to defeating Germany was to isolate and starve them. Great Britain implemented Hankey's idea with a naval blockade. Finding immediate success in keeping Germany's naval fleet confined to port and out of open waters, as well as keeping food and war supplies from arriving into Germany, this blockade lasted throughout the duration of the four-year war.

The date was Tuesday, February 9, 1926. Some ten plus years had passed since the sugar crisis. Sitting alone in his library, Jakob still couldn't put his finger on what he should have done differently as a business owner to avoid all the problems the sugar shortage had caused. Just before 9:00 AM Jakob heard a knock at his front door. His physician had returned to check up on him. Inviting the doctor inside, Jakob happily reported that he was feeling better, but still fatigued. After the examination, the physician said he was pleased with Jakob's steady improvement. Fully aware of his patient's still-weakened state, the doctor recommended that Jakob continue getting additional rest, stay on a steady intake of fluids and to avoid prolonged periods of exposure to the cold weather. Finding these terms agreeable, Jakob thanked his doctor for taking the time to check up on him and bid his doctor farewell.

From early August through late September 1914, the passing of each week saw the price of sugar continue to climb gradually. By the end of September 1914 sugar had climbed to 6.8 cents per pound. "The result of the Great European War was bound to be felt in this country in a great many more ways than the average citizen of the United States realized. That these results should be felt so suddenly and so severely as they have been was not anticipated in any way," the *International Confectioner* tried to explain to its readers in September 1914.

With orders continuing to arrive daily at his Camden factory, Jakob faced a mounting problem that had no quick or easy solution. Still convinced that before long Germany would win a decisive victory against its enemies and that he would soon make up his losses, Jakob went ahead purchasing sugar at the marked-up rate of nearly seventy-five percent. But as the summer of 1914 turned into fall Philadelphia Caramel Company's financial problems became even more dire. Despite producing thousands of pounds of candy daily, company profits kept eroding. Even after raising prices for their signature brands, the confectioner had fallen into the red. It was now time for Jakob to make some very difficult business decisions.

In late 1914 Jakob secured a second mortgage against his candy factory property. He also secured a lien on his vacation property in Colorado. These loans provided the Philadelphia Caramel Company an additional $24,000 to continue its business operations. As a means to save money, Jakob began laying off his work force. From its peak of 250 employees in 1905, one decade later only half that number remained. As conditions worsened, Jakob stopped paying the $500 mortgage payment on the Camden factory. Shuffling between paying off current debt and purchasing additional materials to operate his candy factory, the entire amount of $24,000 was exhausted by the end of 1914. Jakob felt alone and broken. He was more than ready to put the year 1914 behind him.

Every New Year gives hope of a bright future and of achieving new goals. However, as the year 1915 began, the five-month-old war in Europe dulled many such hopes and goals. For Jakob, 1915 began where 1914 left off: his business was in financial turmoil and needed help fast. In desperation he approached one of his leading competitors in the confectionery trade for a loan. Jakob had prior dealings with this particular competitor in the past and shared a common bond with one of the owners, which he hoped would pave the way to a loan.

Henry Brandle and John Smith were well established within the confectionery trade. Forming a partnership in Philadelphia, together they established the Brandle & Smith Company in 1896. For many years the company distinguished itself in the marketplace by the unique glossy finish found exclusively on their brand of hard candies. This company's biggest claim to fame was the widely popular "Satin-Finished" Mellowmint candies.

Like Jakob, John Smith was a gifted engineer turned confectioner. With his knowledge in the machinery field, Smith created and patented many of the devices used in their candy manufacturing plant. As a courtesy to his fellow engineer and competing confectioner, Smith agreed to lend the struggling Philadelphia Caramel Company owner $6,200 with the clear understanding that the entire amount would be paid in full within ninety days. But ninety days later, in March 1915, only seven months into the war, the Philadelphia Caramel Company found itself in deeper financial difficulties. Even after making agreements with its creditors for repayment extensions, the sugar shortage brought on by the war was becoming Jakob's undoing.

Jakob's love and support of Germany was well entrenched, but the German-instigated war had dealt his candy business a severe blow. Throughout 1915 Jakob's company continued to suffer financial losses and by the start of 1916 was in debt to the tune of $66,000. One year later, on February 28, 1916, Jakob received a visit at his factory by a Mr. George Furst. George Furst was an attorney representing the Brandle & Smith Candy Company. Mr. Furst's arrival, although not completely shocking, was nonetheless unexpected. He calmly delivered the sobering news: an equity suit was being filed against the Philadelphia Caramel Company. Of the $66,000 debt total, $37,000 was owed to various creditors, including $5,500 to the Brandle & Smith Company. Suddenly the gravity of the situation struck him. Unable to continue operating his business at a loss, Jakob was now tasked with defending his company in a complaint being filed in the United States District Court in New Jersey.

The March 1, 1916 court complaint read:

> Notwithstanding the fact that every effort has been made to provide funds for the payment of the indebtedness of the Philadelphia Caramel Company, or for the extension of time of payment thereof, such efforts have proved unsuccessful; that unless some definite action is taken…the operation of the plant of the defendant company may be kept intact, great and severe loss will be inflicted on all creditors. [The Philadelphia Caramel Company]has no reasonable hope of finding financial assistance from any quarter to enable it to meet its obligations at the present time.

Immediately following the first court appearance, the Philadelphia Caramel Company fell into receivership. Under orders from Judge John Rellstab, company co-owner and vice president Adolph Ebeling and attorney "Maja" Berry assumed daily operations of the company. Although still the legal owner and responsible for the liabilities of his business, sixty-five-year-old Jakob Schleicher had been, by court order, legally stripped of any decision making pertaining to the operation of his business. His fifteen years making confections were now over.

In the midst of Jakob's personal and business tragedies, he sent his nephew Lewis Mumford a letter. The date was Friday, October 20, 1916 — Lewis' twenty-first birthday. The heartfelt, two-page letter read in part:

> Dear Lewis:
>
> You have entered now into a period of independence and responsibility. You certainly have my best wishes for your body and mental health as well as for a prosperous, successful and honorary career. On this day I would make the wish for [you to have a] good, clean and noble character. While the ignoble may rule in politics, do not cater to the approbation of [these] tendencies. Do your best meanwhile to learn to understand and learn Germany poetry, German literature, ideals, and things pertaining to the practical life and methods of the Germans [as these] will command more respect and interest after the war and it is well to prepare for coming events.

This affectionate letter revealed much about Jakob's state of mind and his outlook. As always, he possessed a certain sparkle of optimism and a hope that better days still lie ahead. Undeterred, Jakob remained confident that a German victory was close at hand and that all would be well soon.

On Friday, January 12, 1917, the day after Germany was to send the secret Zimmermann Telegram to their ambassador in Mexico, a receiver's sale took place on the Philadelphia Caramel Company's premises. As people wandered freely throughout the factory examining the assortment of instruments and tools once used to manufacture sweets, Jakob remembered watching and couldn't help but feel a sense of being encroached upon.

ERIK VARON

RECEIVERS' SALE.

Under the authority of the United States District Court for the District of New Jersey. In the matter of Brandle & Smith Co., a Corporation vs. The Philadelphia Caramel Co., a Corporation.

SAMUEL T. FREEMAN & CO., AUCTIONEERS
ESTABLISHED NOVEMBER 12, 1805

STOCK AND MACHINERY
OF
The Philadelphia Caramel Co.
SECOND ST. and ATLANTIC AVE.
CAMDEN, N. J.

FRIDAY, JANUARY 12, 1917, at 10 A. M.,
ON THE PREMISES.

The sale comprises the Complete Machinery and Stock of The Philadelphia Caramel Co., including Sheridan Power Cutter, Baling Press, Wafer Press and Enrobers, Mixing Kettles, Dough Mixers, 72-inch Melanguer (with revolving bed), Air Compressor, Marshmallow Cutter, Caramel Cutters, Buhse Automatic Kiss Cutters, Caramel Wrapping Machines, Caramel Sizers, Slicers, Sizing Rollers, Candy Pulling Machines, Cooling Tables, Warming Tables, Sugar Mill, Noegat Beating Machine, Gum Cooking Kettle (with gears and stirrer), Copper Kettles, Cream Beater and Cooler, Mogul Starch Buck, Printer and Depositor, Schultz O'Neill Sugar Grinder, Chain Hoist, Motors, Shafting, Pulleys, Tables, Pans, Scales, Trays, Miscellaneous Candy Machinery, Office Fixtures, &c.

☞ *The property will first be offered as a going concern and then in piece-meal lots.*
Sale subject to the confirmation of the Court.
Application for the confirmation of the sale will be made before the United States District Court, for the District of New Jersey, at Newark, N. J., United States District Court Room, Post Office Building, Newark, N. J., on Monday, January 15, 1917, at 10.30 A. M.

By order of Maja L. Berry, } Receivers.
Adolph W. Ebeling,

SAMUEL T. FREEMAN & CO.
AUCTIONEERS
ESTABLISHED NOVEMBER 12, 1805
NOS. 1519-21 CHESTNUT STREET
PHILADELPHIA, PA.

Public notice advising of Philadelphia Caramel Company's receivers' sale.

JAKOB'S STORY AND THE AMERICAN DREAM

Just before the sale got underway, one final meeting took place among the auction curator, George Freeman from the Samuel T. Freeman Auction House, attorneys Maja Berry and George Furst, Philadelphia Caramel's co-receiver, Adolph Ebeling and a downcast Jakob Schleicher. The discussion of this meeting entailed the exact auction procedures and what could be expected as the auction progressed.

At 10:00 AM the bidding began with all property being offered in bulk to the highest bidder. Within just a few minutes the starting bid of $15,000 escalated to its highest offer of $15,750. Next, all 397 lots were auctioned individually with the stipulation that the outcome of the auction would be based on whichever portion reached the highest total: the bulk sales price or the individual lots sales price.

As the auctioneer proceeded to guide the group of fifty to sixty people from room to room methodically auctioning off each item one by one, Jakob could only watch helplessly. His former company was being sold piecemeal to the highest bidder. It felt like everything he had built, from the plant itself to his business relationships and creative customer engagement schemes, was being disassembled piece by piece. The auction proceeded at a crawl over the next several hours. By the time the last bid was placed on the final item, the total amount realized had reached $19,000.

Following the auction, one local Philadelphia newspaper headline read "Big Candy Company Plant Forced to Close Because Of Sugar Shortage." In the article, a representative from the Brandle & Smith Candy Company explained that besides the debt that was owed them, a business rationale for the lawsuit against the Philadelphia Caramel Company existed. "We were all looking for [sugar]. That is why the famine hit us so hard. We had none stored ahead."

With his days of being an engineer and confectioner now over, Jakob tried to make sense of his losses. Over the course of the next two years, in between the ongoing court hearings that sorted out various legal matters, Jakob closely monitored the progress of the war. Reading the news accounts, he continued to cheer for Germany to defeat the Allies. While regularly reminded of his company's demise, Jakob eventually came to accept that, even had the candy company been able to stay afloat, he no longer had the energy required to operate a business on a day-to-day basis.

By 1917, much like his beloved Germany, Jakob had dealt with his own battles and felt the crush of having lost his "empire." With the death of his wife, the closing of his candy business and the lawsuit that followed, in many ways Jakob too had been through a war. As he concluded the sixth section of his memoir, the title of this portion seemed appropriate: "Losing Everything."

As a lover of poetry, and in a way only few others could relate to, Jakob affirmed Oscar Wilde's famous words: "The heart was made to be broken."

Following the demise of his candy business, Jakob did manage to find one way to keep himself useful during the solitariness of his retirement years.

CHAPTER 15

Jakob's Declining Years

*He who would pass his declining years
with honor and comfort,
should, when young, consider
that he may one day become old,
and remember when he is old, that he has once been young."*
—Joseph Addison, poet

Wednesday, February 10, 1926. This day marked a turning point for Jakob Schleicher. His health, which had rebounded nicely, took an abrupt turn. The flu-like symptoms and the dehydration he had been battling over the past few weeks had unexpectedly worsened overnight. Upon waking, his entire body ached and he felt considerably weaker. Believing he was still getting over his cold and that he simply needed more rest, Jakob remained in bed and slept through most of the day. He kept a pad of paper and a pen close at hand. Weak and tired, but aware he was nearing the end of his memoir, Jakob managed to write down a few thoughts during his waking intervals. These notes outlined the significant events that had taken place during his life following the closure of his candy business.

Following the receiver's sale and closure of his candy company in January 1917, spring arrived, bringing with it more conflict in the world and to Jakob Schleicher.

In early 1917, hostilities in the European War sharply escalated when Germany announced plans to resume unrestricted submarine warfare. Just as was forewarned, in February and March 1917 the number of ships sunk by German U-boats spiked to over 500. Included in this figure were merchant ships flying the American flag. As a result, merchant ships traveling across the Atlantic destined for British ports saw the number of successful deliveries drop by a staggering seventy-five percent.

During the early part of 1917, Germany's war of words with America also sharpened. A mocking chant popular with Germans went, "America cannot swim. They cannot fly. They will not come." But as America's involvement in the war drew closer, the United States became strongly divided over the conflict. Some felt entering the fray would tip the decision of the war in the Allies' favor and would lead to an Allied victory. Others felt American deaths in a European conflict were unwarranted and unnecessary. The slogan "I didn't raise my boy to be a soldier," was a growing sentiment.

Demographic statistics in 1917 revealed 8 million of America's 103 million citizens—nearly eight percent—had either German parents or German grandparents. Virtually no German-American citizens called for intervention. Rather, most spoke highly of their German culture and called for neutrality.

After all, they reasoned, German-Americans had a strong influence on American culture. Americans had adopted various facets of the German lifestyle including early childhood education (kindergarten), music and philosophy as well as such things like sausage, pilsner-style beer, and the Hamburg steak (later hamburger). Even more important, however, was the key role German-Americans played in America's economy with its contribution to its workforce. Germany was aware of the large German-American population in the United States and tried to use them to their advantage. In fact, since the beginning of the war many thousands of German-American citizens had attempted to enlist in the German army to show loyalty to their homeland. For those who weren't ready to take a step that drastic, Germany directed propaganda toward German-Americans and managed to turn a small portion of that population against America.

Attacks on American soil by German agents were occurring with more frequency. Specifically targeted was a munitions depot, Black Tom Island in New Jersey, which housed 900 tons of ammunition destined to go to the Allies. This attack was followed by an incident involving one Heinrich Albert, who was assigned to the German embassy in Washington D.C. Albert inadvertently left his briefcase on a New York City subway car. When it was revealed that the briefcase contained evidence that German sympathizers had planned various acts of sabotage to undermine American interests, a wave of anger and a gradual breaking of relations with Germany ensued.

For Jakob, the spring of 1917 was painfully uncertain. Since his wife's passing in 1914, the anniversary of her death every subsequent March was a difficult time of year for him. With her gone, and with the failure of his business, he had lost his anchor and mooring. On top of those losses, the bankruptcy and unresolved debts overwhelmed him. He had found some certainty in following the war, but recent developments on that front brought him nothing but more emotional turmoil. At times he found even simple decisions impossible to make; it seemed he was losing his balance.

By 1917, Adolph Ebeling and his wife were parents of four children. Jakob felt a sense of responsibility for his stepson, and hated being the reason Adolph no longer had gainful employment. Deeply bothered that Adolph could not financially support his own family, Jakob decided to rectify the situation as best he could.

Quietly Jakob also faced an internal struggle. Since coming to America, Jakob had overseen the operation of two very successful businesses. Even with his positive track record, intelligence and all of the schooling and professional training he'd had to become an engineer, Jakob worried about his reputation. What did people think of him after losing his candy business to bankruptcy? He struggled, thinking that somehow he had failed as a businessman. He felt in some way that the bankruptcy was a personal reflection of him and the Schleicher name. In light of the war, he also worried that his business failures reflected negatively on his German heritage.

In May 1917, as America was preparing to send the first wave of soldiers to Europe, Jakob insisted on spending half the money he had set aside for his retirement to establish a new business for his stepson's benefit.

For no other reason than to help his stepson, Jakob established the South Camden Terminal and Industrial Realty Company. This new business rented space out from the former Philadelphia Caramel candy plant to paying tenants. Adolph

Ebeling became the property manager who oversaw the lease of over 40,000 square feet of warehouse space for the purpose of manufacturing and storage of goods. Happily, the new business opened additional opportunities for Jakob and his stepson.

In mid-June 1917, new tenants George Townsend Jr., A. M. Haley and Charles Bush established the Cecil Candy and Chocolate Company. Adopting the slogan "Quality Without Thrills," the new confectioners sought someone with Adolph Ebeling's level of experience as a company secretary and as a recognized expert in the candy manufacturing field. They hired him, both as a consultant and as their company secretary.

With Adolph now comfortably settled in his new career, Jakob struggled to find things to do to fill his own empty schedule. Within a few months, however, Jakob had found a solution.

"When finally his candy business went bankrupt, he spent his declining years as night watchman [at] the [candy] plant he once owned," nephew Lewis Mumford remembered. Although quite different from before, being a night watchman at the old candy factory did have its benefits. Jakob no longer had the responsibilities associated with operating a business. More importantly, however, this position gave Jakob a sense of value and made him feel useful once again. Access to the factory provided Jakob the emotional connection he needed at the time. The same factory he had known for almost twelve years, now included a watchman's service in the rental agreement for all new tenants. Jakob also decided that with the income he made in renting out the facility, he would begin the slow process of paying back the debts he inherited from the bankruptcy.

On July 4, 1917 the first wave of American troops known as "Dough Boys" arrived in Boulogne, France. Just as France and

Marquis de Lafayette had come to the rescue of America 140 years earlier during the American Revolution, it was now America's turn to aid France in their time of need. Fittingly, America's slogan became "Lafayette, we are here." Averaging 300,000 new arrivals every month, the American Expeditionary Forces in Europe grew rapidly. General John Pershing called upon all Americans to be vigilant as their country entered the war. "Three thousand miles from home, an American army is fighting for you. Everything you hold worthwhile is at stake. Only the hardest blows can win against the enemy we are fighting. Invoking the spirit of our forefathers, the army asks your unshrinking support to the end that the high ideals for which America stands may endure upon the Earth." But even after the United States and his own nephew Lewis Mumford joined the war, Jakob stubbornly continued to support the German cause, going so far as to send pro-German pamphlets to his nephew at the naval posts where he served. This extreme behavior risked both Mumford's and Jakob's safety. It was yet another demonstration of Jakob's emotional state and frame of mind at the time. "If inquiry were made and had they searched my bedroom at home in New York, they would have found a whole stack of pro-German pamphlets which my Uncle Jakob had sent me earlier in the war," Lewis Mumford confessed.

President Teddy Roosevelt coined the phrase "hyphenated Americans" to refer to Jakob and others who gave other national or ethnic names equal footing with their American identity. The typical practice at the time was to call oneself German-American, Italian-American and so on, using a hyphen to connect the descriptors. "A hyphenated American is not an American at all…the only man who is a good American is the man who is an American and nothing else," Roosevelt claimed. Although Roosevelt's intent was to break down distinctions—i.e., that by dropping any other nationality prefixes all Americans would feel a stronger sense of belonging and unity—his statement instead caught fire. The press soon began referring to all German-Americans as "hyphens." "One against another...this awful war should not be made more terrible by internecine strife," one newspaper boldly rebutted at the time. But people who held the more inclusive view were in the minority. America's internal division failed to stop with the squabble over hyphens.

President Woodrow Wilson followed up President Roosevelt's remarks by proclaiming all German citizens residing in America as "alien enemies." Wilson then quickly issued two sets of regulations imposing restrictions on German-born males residing in America. Soon, 250,000 German-Americans were required to register at their local post office and carry registration cards. As a result of the Espionage Act of 1917 and the Sedition Act of 1918, two thousand German-Americans were also viewed by the government as being dangerous enough to be incarcerated in internment camps for the duration of the war. In April 1918, former Senator Lafayette Young of Iowa was quoted as stating "We have more trouble with preachers who preach in German than with anybody else. They are Huns propaganda machines whether they intend it or not. There are 5000 persons in Iowa who ought to be in the stockade this very minute. The nest eggs of all treason in the United States is the German language and German press, I am in favor of cleaning up America now. This is our country." Seemingly unfazed by the possible consequences, Jakob's view of Germany held firm. In his memoir, Jakob also revealed his opinion of President Roosevelt: "Roosevelt begins to talk in German and as an educated man is not ashamed to use the dative case instead of the accusative case, saying: I am pleased to welcome them (Germans). —Such a fraud may get votes of illiterates but history will give him his right dues."

Friday, February 12, 1926 was a day best described with an image of sand rushing toward the bottom of the hourglass. In a matter of days, Jakob's health declined rapidly. The chills, the sweating, the low body temperature and the listlessness all factored into the pale appearance and weakened state that he was now in. Jakob's breathing also changed, becoming more labored and shallow. Before calling the physician back for another house call, Jakob had someone else he needed to call first—his nephew, Lewis Mumford. Jakob's memoir meanwhile deteriorated as a result of his lassitude. Entries were less detailed, less legible, fewer in number.

As American troops began to see action in Europe, back home President Woodrow Wilson was working on a solution to address the humanitarian crisis taking place in Europe. In Russia alone food shortages resulted in nearly 750,000 malnutrition deaths over the four years of fighting. In the summer of 1917 President Wilson established the Food Administration. Its top administrator, Herbert Hoover, adopted the slogan "Food will win the war." While countries such as Britain and France had implemented policies for rationing their food supply, Germany appeared to have made an oversight in this regard. Their hardship was severe. If war was about using all of one's resources, Germany's failure to ration food clearly demonstrated a serious error in prioritization. Believing victory would come to the country that had a larger food supply, the United States undertook a rationing effort on a voluntary basis, but not without a rousing national campaign. American collectively reduced their food consumption by fifteen percent in the first year of Gasless

Sundays, Meatless Mondays, and Wheatless Wednesdays. These additional resources were then distributed to the Allies. Meanwhile, as their food supplies were dwindling, unrest and revolt shook most European countries, including Germany. Enduring years of war and food shortages without complaining had taken its toll as unrest, walkouts and protests swept across Europe. While these protests didn't call for the end of fighting, the protestors demanded an end to the hardships, degradation and senseless sacrifice they continued to make. Food was in fact becoming the answer to winning the war.

In the spring of 1918, Germany launched its largest attack since the start of the war. Its troops advanced to within sixty miles of Paris. With the Allies reaching a near breaking point, by July Germany had made a final push to win the war. But General Erich Ludendorff erred—he failed to adequately plan for reinforcements or materials to arrive at the front line—and although the Allies sustained massive casualties, they managed to fend off Germany's final offensive. "Everything I had feared had become a reality. Our war machine was no longer efficient even though the great majority of divisions still fought heroically," Ludendorff conceded.

On August 8, 1918 an Allied effort known as Hundred Days Offensive launched. General Ludendorff described this date as the "black day of the German army." By the end of September 1918 the Allies had regained momentum. Suffering a psychological blow when the Allies broke through the Germans' reinforced "Hindenburg Line," Germany went on the retreat. General Ludendorff decided that, while his military still had some level of fighting ability left, an armistice should quickly be reached with the Allies. But American General John Pershing did not want Germany returning home under the belief the war ended in a draw.

General Pershing felt strongly that an Allied victory was in sight. He was determined to defeat Germany and finish the job America had started. Before General Pershing had the opportunity to defeat Germany, however, an armistice was signed on November 11, 1918. At 11:00 AM on the 1,568th day of fighting the entire battlefield fell silent. One soldier remarked, "It was the most remarkable day in the history of the world."

General Ludendorff later provided this analysis: "The history of the German people is concluded for the moment by the peace. The future lies dark before us. All delusions have vanished. We look into nothingness." But for the German soldiers who had made the trenches their home over the past four years, a different attitude emerged. They quickly adopted the motto, "Better an end with terror than terror without end."

America's soldiers emerged from the war as heroes; America was viewed as the greatest and strongest country on Earth. The British praised America as "the last great reserve army of civilization," while the French described America's intervention as "the magical operation of a blood transfusion." In reality the Allied victory owed just as much to German exhaustion and hunger as to any other factor.

In surveying the carnage the war had left behind, America's ambassador in London, Walter Hines Page, wrote, "The hills above Verdun are not blown to pieces worse than the whole social structure and the intellectual and spiritual life of Europe." There was hope that the Great War would be the war to end all wars, and, for the moment, peace had in fact returned in Europe.

Upon conclusion of the war in November 1918, Jakob was ten days away from celebrating his sixty-seventh birthday. Remembering how he was about to enter his golden years alone, he concluded this session by quoting the words of poet Joseph

JAKOB'S STORY AND THE AMERICAN DREAM

Addison: "He who would pass his declining years with honor and comfort, should, when young, consider that he may one day become old, and remember when he is old, that he has once been young."

Having once been young, it was now time for Jakob to journey through his declining years — in solitude, hopefully with some measurable amount of comfort and a degree of honor as well.

CHAPTER 16

The Clock Winds Down

In your calm is your strength.
-German proverb

Valentine's Day 1926 was a Sunday. While many Americans were attending church services and expressing admiration to their sweethearts, the atmosphere at the home in which Jakob Schleicher rented a room was melancholy and surreal. Jakob's perception of time had changed; time seemed to have ground to a halt. Those who visited him that day felt much the same. Over the past day and a half much had taken place. Having learned that his stepfather was extremely ill, Adolph, his wife and his children arrived to tend to Jakob. Jakob's doctor had also been summoned.

Well aware of the recent history of dehydration and flu-like symptoms Mr. Schleicher had been dealing with over the past several weeks, even the doctor was startled to see how rapidly

Jakob's health had deteriorated. With extreme care, the doctor assessed and surveyed his patient's symptoms. Jakob had a severe case of pneumonia; worse, his heart rate was dropping. Pulling Adolph aside, the doctor explained the seriousness of the situation. Jakob's body was now being put through its toughest challenge yet. In his frail state there was no guarantee he would pull through. After the doctor advised the family to closely monitor Jakob and to keep him in an upright position while in bed, he nodded for Adolph to step into the hallway. Once outside, the doctor bowed his head and compassionately but honestly explained that Jakob's outcome was now up to whether or not he could fight off the pneumonia. He recommended to Adolph that now might be a good time to summon Jakob's extended family—just in case. Hearing this, Adolph quickly understood the gravity of the situation. The physician quietly went back inside and gathered his equipment. Looking at his long-time patient, the doctor paused as if to say his final goodbye to an old friend. After a brief moment, he turned and exited the room. As they began walking toward the front door, the doctor told Adolph that he would return if asked, but for now there was nothing else he could do. Having difficulty digesting the information he was just given, Adolph saw the doctor out the door and in a state of bewilderment, closed the front door. Sensing the end was approaching, Adolph, who usually did not display his emotions openly, turned to his wife who was standing nearby and without saying a word, hugged her. Adolph advised his wife of the doctor's diagnosis and carefully went over the doctor's recommendations and instructions. Still in shock and disbelief, Adolph returned to check up on Jakob, who was resting comfortably in bed, completely unaware of how ill he truly was.

JAKOB'S STORY AND THE AMERICAN DREAM

A short time later, as Adolph sat next to his stepfather, there was a knock at the front door. Adolph recognized a familiar voice coming from the living room. Leaving Jakob's side momentarily, Adolph entered the living room and was relieved to see that his cousin Lewis Mumford had arrived. The two men knew each other well. "Adolph, was, until I was twenty, one of my legal guardians," Mumford later recounted. "On our occasional meetings, [Cousin Adolph] had a way of tactfully slipping me a greenback when we said [our] goodbyes," Lewis fondly added. But like other passing memories, those days seemed long past now. Today was a day to focus on Jakob. After greeting each other warmly, the conversation turned sober. Once again out of earshot from Jakob, Adolph explained the doctor's diagnosis to Lewis, adding that other family members were also on their way. In preparing Lewis for what he was about to see, Adolph advised that although Jakob's physical health was failing, mentally he was still alert and coherent. Adolph then guided Lewis up the stairwell and into Jakob's bedroom.

In the final few notations of his memoir, Jakob wrote about the war and what the conflict meant to him as a German-American. The "war to end all wars" had left death and destruction on a scale never before seen by mankind. Those who initially believed the risks of starting a war were worth the potential gains probably never grasped how catastrophic it would turn out to be. In just over four years of fighting an estimated total of nine million soldiers had been killed. Then, with the war winding down, an influenza epidemic broke out. Jakob recounted how, in an almost apocalyptic manner, an additional twenty million people around the globe died as a result of this outbreak.

With Germany having lost two million soldiers to the war and thousands more citizens to hunger, Jakob wondered, *what good did all of this suffering do, and what did it all mean?* To start, people on each side of the conflict recognized the dead and proclaimed them heroes. Like many others, Jakob believed those who fought, as well as those who struggled back home in Germany during the war, did so honorably. As the German adage went, "More enemies, more honor." The people of Germany had displayed honor, Jakob felt, for fighting against virtually all of Europe, not to mention America. Germany battled valiantly and had held its own without being defeated or surrendering. Many pro-German supporters, including Jakob, were convinced that with more time Germany could have won the war had the armistice not been signed.

Like many who had supported Germany during the war, Jakob believed Germany never lost the war. An armistice, after all, was an agreement by both sides of the conflict to cease fighting in order for peace to return. Although the Allies had taken control at the time the armistice was agreed upon, neither side had declared itself victorious immediately after the war. It was only after the Treaty of Versailles was signed in June 1919 that America and the Allies claimed victory. As if motivated by greed rather than the actual terms of the treaty, leaders of Allied nations acted to punish Germany as they brokered the peace. France, Britain and America demanded that Germany pay $33 billion in reparations. Germany was forced to surrender previously occupied territories, forming new countries such as Czechoslovakia and Poland, thus bringing about a new landscape in Europe. Germany was also forced to surrender their navy fleet and disarm their military. Then, under the threat that the Allies would resume the war, Germany was forced to sign a

"War Guilt Clause" admitting that the start of the war was due to German aggression.

Like most Germans of the period, Jakob believed that the Treaty of Versailles was illegitimate and never accepted the Allies' contention that Germany had lost the war. Lewis Mumford remembered while "Woodrow Wilson, in his evangelical postwar tour of Europe, was spontaneously hailed as a living savior by the crowds that greeted him everywhere," his uncle Jakob railed against how the armistice was turned into an unfair and humiliating settlement against Germany. This was one of the few times that Lewis and Jakob were in agreement as they both denounced the Versailles Treaty as an assault on the very fiber of President Wilson's original pleas for a fair and lasting peace.

In addition, Jakob was disillusioned by how the American people and government had treated German-Americans during the war. The hostility they displayed—everything ranging from the derisive label, "Hun," used to describe anyone with German heritage, to some German-Americans being held prisoner during the war—all the way up to America's overall involvement in Europe's affairs, Jakob found unsettling and disheartening. To make matters worse, Jakob observed that while capitalists basked in America's ability to produce mass amounts of military and industrial goods, they simultaneously discriminated against immigrants from Europe—the very people who could help boost production and money-making to ever higher levels. Not only was Jakob put off by this pervasive anti-European feeling, but as a longtime *American* citizen, he personally found this treatment to be confusing and embarrassing. This was not the same America that had warmly greeted him upon his arrival to Philadelphia in 1876. Even eight years after the war, Jakob still struggled to make sense of this unfair and unjust treatment toward newcomers.

As Lewis Mumford entered Jakob's bedroom that Sunday afternoon he observed his uncle in bed with pillows propping him up in a seated position. His uncle's usually well-kempt gray hair was in disarray and he appeared to have gone unshaven for several days. Lewis couldn't help but notice the pallor and the bags under Jakob's eyes. This condition was so out of character for Jakob that Lewis struggled to register the man in the bed as even being his uncle. In a gentle voice, Adolph woke Jakob and told him that he had a visitor. Adolph then left the room allowing the two to talk alone.

As they had done so many times in the past, Jakob and Lewis engaged each other in conversation. This time, however, their discussion did not last hours. Lewis noticed that his uncle became winded after visiting for only a few minutes. Realizing this might be his final opportunity to visit his uncle, Lewis asked if there was anything Jakob needed or wanted. Jakob said yes.

Moments later Lewis summoned Adolph back into the bedroom and explained that Jakob had a request. With the help of Lewis and Adolph, Jakob wanted to return to his library. Initially, both men tried to talk Jakob into staying in bed, but as Jakob insisted, they eventually agreed to escort him out of bed and into his library. Slowly these two men supported the old and frail family patriarch, half-carrying him, and sat him down at his desk. Upon Jakob's request, Lewis powered on the radiola. Jakob sat motionless, taking in the scenery, the sounds and the company of his two closest relatives.

Moments later Jakob called Lewis to his side. Jakob explained that located in a drawer of his desk was the memoir he had been working on over the past couple of months. A corresponding pad of paper was also in his bedroom. Jakob admitted to Lewis that he knew a couple of months back that he didn't have much time remaining, so he decided to pen a memoir in an effort to leave something behind. Jakob said he hoped his memoir would prove useful to someone, providing insight into his life, his view of the world, as well as his unique American experience. Jakob's only request was that it not be read until his passing. Lewis agreed to honor the request, assuring him that the memoir would not be handled until that time. A mere five minutes had passed since Jakob first arrived in his office. His poor health and weakened state, however, did not permit him to remain there any longer. He was then gently escorted back ito his room where he returned to bed. Exhausted, he immediately fell asleep.

Following his thoughts on the war, Jakob's memoir briefly went over his retirement years beginning in May 1919.

It was just weeks before the treaty summit at Versailles was scheduled to get underway that the Cecil Candy and Chocolate Company failed. Its demise was attributed to the collapse of the sugar market. Immediately after the war ended, the price of sugar had dropped drastically. Many confectioners, who were fearful that the price of sugar would continue to rise, had signed contracts during the war to purchase sugar at a fixed rate. Forced to pay these higher sugar prices following the war, companies such as the Cecil Candy and Chocolate Company, along with Philadelphia confectioner Hershey's, struggled to stay in business. Whereas Hershey managed to weather this storm, the Cecil Candy and Chocolate Company did not.

Cecil's closure affected Jakob in two ways. First, his night watchman position ended, along with the small income stream it had afforded. Second, Jakob now had to find a new tenant. Unable to locate one, Jakob could no longer pay the mortgage on the property, so the South Camden Terminal and Industrial

Realty Company closed for business. Sixty-eight-year-old Jakob Schleicher was forced to sell his former candy manufacturing plant in Camden. He was now ready to spend his final years permanently retired.

In the final entry of his memoir, which by that time was barely legible, Jakob touched on the variety of recreational and leisure activities that kept him busy during those past few years. These included solitary projects such as gardening, reading and writing. He also wrote of his attempts to reestablish a relationship with his first love, Elvina Baron.

"To the end, every week, he would send long letters and tender poems to my mother," Lewis Mumford recounted. "He would work in his garden in season, minding his beloved roses; and he would read the fables of La Fontaine and the other classics of his youth," Mumford added. There was one additional past time Jakob enjoyed during his retirement: reading *The Dial*. Lewis Mumford was associate director of the periodical, but Jakob read it for reasons besides family loyalty. *The Dial* frequently turned down the work of up and coming American authors like Ernest Hemingway in favor of contributions from better known European authors of the day. Not put off by the aesthetic experiments, or by the magazine's political radicalism, Jakob read *The Dial* regularly with deep appreciation of its excellent literary criticism, even submitting pieces for publication on a few occasions.

Monday, February 15, 1926 was a quiet and melancholy day as Jakob's family prepared for the inevitable. With his heart rate dropping steadily, it was now just a matter of hours before his passing would occur. As his family held a round-the-clock vigil, they each watched helplessly as his chest tightened with every breath he took. Meanwhile, a few visitors trickled in throughout the day to say their goodbyes, including Jakob's landlord and his family. The husband and wife each expressed their gratitude for Jakob being their tenant, and for having shared a little piece of his life with them. The husband, who was aware of Jakob's German background, left Jakob and his relatives with an old German proverb: "In your calm is your strength." While he was going to miss his stepson, his grandchildren, and his nephew, falling back onto his Reformed Protestant faith, Jakob was calm and was now prepared for the afterlife.

Tuesday, February 16, 1926 brought one final visitor to Jakob's home: Elvina Baron.

As if Jakob had been holding on to see her, his tired eyes sparkled as she walked into his bedroom. He could feel fluid building up in his lungs, and could barely breathe, but was nonetheless pleased to see Elvina. Mrs. Baron, now sixty-one, walked in and kissed Jakob on his forehead. She then sat down on the bed next to him. She was as attractive as ever; the gray hairs gracefully showed her age. Elvina had never forgotten meeting Jakob in 1881. After her aunt sent her back home to New York that summer, these two lives continued on their own separate ways. Losing contact was painful for both of them. Now, all these years later, taking him by his hands and seeing him in this condition, Elvina could not help but get choked up—in part for the dreams that were never realized, but also with pity for his failing health. Holding his listless hands, seeing his parched lips and pale skin and looking into his tired eyes, she knew the end was drawing near. She spent the next several minutes sharing with him those final things she meant to tell him but hadn't until now.

Then, it was Jakob's turn. Barely able to speak, he recited a quote from German poet, Angelus Silesius, "Each of us has inside of us the image of what we ought to become. Until that has been realized, our happiness is not perfect." Admitting to her that he never achieved what he desired most, marrying her, he uttered "I make this late confession in the hope that it will bring me forgiveness, putting a quietus on the stings of conscience for that lapse of my youth." For the first time, he opened up and told her something he had never told anyone: his inner struggle between his stoic sense of duty versus his personal desire. Thinking back to when his closest friend, August Ebeling, was on his death bed, Jakob shared with Elvina the request August had made. Knowing he was about to die, August pleaded with Jakob to look after his wife and son. At that moment, seeing his friend dying, Jakob made a life-altering decision. He agreed and promised his friend he would fulfill his wishes, even though it would cost him his relationship with Elvina Baron.

Unaware he had ever had this conversation with her uncle, Elvina broke down in tears. Jakob soon followed. While still heartbroken, at that moment Elvina acquired a newfound respect for the man she had always loved. Regardless, all the two could do now was to sit together speechless, no doubt wishing their lives would have merged long ago.

Just after 7:00 PM Jakob told Elvina he was tired and he was ready to go home. Preparing for his final moments, Elvina called her son and the rest of the family into the bedroom. Jakob's family reassured him that he had completed his work here and sadly said their goodbyes. A few moments later as he ebbed between life and eternity, Elvina took his hand and told him that she would always love him. Jakob whispered "Elvina" and breathed his last breath.

Everyone in the bedroom was in tears as Jakob passed away. Some who heard Jakob's final word felt sure Jakob's wife was welcoming him into the afterlife. Elvina Baron, however, was convinced Jakob had said goodbye to her one final time.

CHAPTER 17

Lewis Mumford's Closing Thoughts

Every heart that has beat strong and cheerfully has left a hopeful impulse behind it in the world, and bettered the tradition of mankind.
— Robert Louis Stevenson, Scottish poet

Following Jakob's death, newspapers such as the *Camden Courier* and the *Philadelphia Inquirer* notified their readers of this one-time industrialist's passing. A few weeks later, those in the confectionery community were informed of his death when the *Confectioner's Journal* wrote a tribute about the Philadelphia Caramel Company's founder. "No doubt several of his old friends will be sorry to learn of his passing," a portion of the tribute stated.

In keeping with his Reformed Protestant faith, Jakob had no church service or formal funeral. On Thursday evening, however, two days after his death, friends were invited to call and express their condolences to his family.

Among those who contacted Jakob's family that evening was John Smith, the engineer turned confectioner from the Brandle & Smith Company. Although Mr. Smith and Jakob were, for many years, business competitors, they had developed a mutual friendship following the 1916 lawsuit. Expressing sorrow over the loss of his friend, Smith offered to pay for the funeral expenses. While his gesture spoke volumes about the level of respect these two men had developed for each other, the family politely declined his offer.

Three days after his death a small, private graveside service was held for Jakob at Arlington Cemetery in Merchantville, New Jersey. After the minister finished his brief homily, Jakob was interred next to his wife, Elvina. That same afternoon the family hosted a celebration of Jakob Scleicher's life at his stepson's home.

Flowers and an array of photos forming a collage of Jakob's life welcomed those who arrived at the home. In a fitting tribute, Jakob's cherished radiola was removed from his library and situated in Adolph's living room where it played music in the background for the guests.

Among those in attendance that day were a few close family friends and neighbors, a small handful of former employees from the Philadelphia Caramel candy factory and Jakob's landlord, who briefly dropped in to pay their respects. Grieving family members, including Mr. and Mrs. Adolph Ebeling, their four children, along with Elvina Baron and her adult son, Lewis Mumford, were also in attendance.

The few dozen people who were present took this opportunity to exchange personal stories and memorable interactions

JAKOB'S STORY AND THE AMERICAN DREAM

they each had with Jakob. One notable tribute that day came from one of Jakob's grandsons, James Ebeling.

Twenty-year-old James Ebeling spoke in front of the entire group of guests who had gathered at the house that afternoon. After introducing himself and explaining proudly that he was named after his grandfather, James read from a prepared statement. "Looking back, I realize more and more how much I owe to this very intelligent and humane man. Uncle James as he was called by most of [the older] generation — to us he was simply Grandpa," James explained.

After reciting a couple of personal stories in the form of a fond encomium, James ended by sharing the lasting image he had of his late grandfather. "I can still close my eyes and see him sitting in his little office in Camden pecking out stories on his ancient typewriter," he told the gathering. They applauded warmly, in part for James's heartfelt and carefully thought out words, but also to acknowledge Jakob and the legacy he left behind.

As he had promised, Lewis Mumford did not handle his uncle's memoir until Jakob's passing. In fact, it was not until late that evening, after everyone had left Adolph's home, that Lewis returned to his uncle's library and quietly read the memoir. Although he had come to know his uncle deeply, having spent numerous occasions in meaningful conversation with Jakob, reflecting on the memoir, Lewis's admiration of his uncle grew even more.

Reading the memoir gave Mumford a more intimate perspective on how Jakob viewed the world and how it translated into the person he had become. Going over the sections that detailed the personal struggles Jakob had endured, Lewis came to realize just how vulnerable — how human — his uncle truly was.

Lewis Mumford. Photo courtesy Granger, NYC.

During his return trip to New York, Lewis began reflecting on both his uncle and the memoir. He asked himself the following three questions:
1. What was the significance of Jakob Schleicher's life?
2. How did Jakob change the world?
3. What was his uncle's legacy and how should his uncle be remembered?

As if taking on a personal challenge, Lewis spent the next several days contemplating how to answer each question. He wondered *how a man's life could be summarized in a few short answers.* Having a uniquely close relationship with his uncle, and now feeling like a confidant of sorts, Lewis Mumford was up to the challenge as only the right person could be. Carefully considering each of Jakob's personal characteristics and the various contributions his uncle made, not only in the engine and confectionery fields, but also as an American and an innovator who made the most of every opportunity he was given, Lewis painstakingly crafted an answer to each question.

Observing that his uncle grappled with the aging process, Lewis began by noting that Jakob Schleicher's life was significant—even unto his uncle's very last breath. In engineering terms, Jakob's life, in many ways it seemed, had run out of gas and stalled. Unable to propel himself forward ever since his wife's passing, Lewis described this senectitude season of his uncle's life as not being for the faint at heart. Nonetheless, Lewis delved into his uncle's single most notable characteristic, his innocence. Or perhaps a better description was the degree of naïveté his uncle possessed throughout his life, which provided some level of resiliency. Beginning with the innocence of his youth and the magic of that particular Easter morning and continuing through his golden years, Lewis noted the quixotic view Jakob held toward Germany and the war. Jakob was a believer in all things, a humanist, and at the core, an optimist, Lewis wrote. This characteristic did not detract from his intelligence or complexity. Rather, it was a trait that made him more human and more likeable to everyone he met. "His pure blue eyes had a sparkling innocence that never left them," Mumford once again recited.

As Jakob's classical education built the essence of the person, Lewis felt that, out of the many life experiences his uncle wrote about in his memoir and shared with him over the years, there was one event from his uncle's youth, above all others, that was the most influential and pivotal. This one event, Lewis believed, had made the deepest impression—for a couple of reasons.

Jakob's patriotism toward Prussia and his enlightenment as to the meaning of independence, liberty and freedom began to sprout after touring the battlefield at Waterloo. To start, his uncle's view of Prussia was elevated. The pride of being of German descent not only was passed down to him at an early age, but on that particular excursion, his view was transcended as he learned about Prussia's war hero, Field Marshal von Blücher coming to rescue the Seventh Coalition. As Jakob saw it, Prussia was not only his family's place of origin, but soon his view changed to include this nation being a force for good in the world. His view of the Fatherland gradually became more pronounced after his wife's passing.

It was also at Waterloo that Jakob first learned about independence and liberty. Lewis firmly believed that, as his uncle traversed the battlefield that day, he came to discover that liberty was more than just personal freedom; liberty was a gift to be treasured. This expedition was but the first of many lessons in Jakob's life on this subject. His uncle's journey to America in 1876 had indeed become the place where Jakob experienced firsthand the independence and liberty he learned about while touring Waterloo's battlefield.

Upon Jakob's arrival in the United States, Lewis described how his uncle discovered two profound truths. The first was that liberty guarantees all Americans—regardless of their sex, religious belief or race—independence and freedom. Next, Lewis noted the meaning of the adage "whoever wishes to be free, must not only eat the fruits of the tree of liberty, but also water its roots" in Jakob's life. This idea was the bedrock of Jakob's success in America. Jakob seized the opportunity to

JAKOB'S STORY AND THE AMERICAN DREAM

play a small but significant role in America's industrialization era. Mimicking his uncle Eugen's ability to visualize countless possibilities, Jakob manufactured and sold dynamos, helping power the first form of electric lighting in America. This was a very tangible achievement that Lewis was proud to highlight.

On the subject of liberty, Lewis Mumford added that his uncle had been part of a special generation that saw the arrival of the Statue of Liberty in America. In the same manner that Lady Liberty's torch would symbolically become a beacon of light to those around the world, Lewis believed his uncle displayed his own *beacon of light*, which burnt brightest during and after World War I. Although Lewis himself questioned Jakob's sentiment toward America somewhat, he observantly noted Jakob's American loyalty went hand in hand with his uncle's core values and ideals, both of which remained strong. During this difficult and stressful period in world history, as the opinions and beliefs of some Americans swayed with the current of the times, Jakob's view of liberty had never wavered. Deeply troubled as he read, witnessed and experienced the hostility towards German-Americans, Jakob held firm that these individuals deserved an equal amount of liberty and freedom. They were American citizens, after all. Jakob felt strongly that the imprisonment of German-Americans and the derisive labels applied to them was not only un-American, it was also morally wrong. "Life without liberty is like a body without spirit," Lewis remembered his uncle occasionally quoting from the poet and philosopher, Kahlil Gibran.

Continuing, Lewis Mumford then explained why and how he felt his uncle changed the world, or at the very least, his corner of it. Mumford explained that we all traverse the obstacle course called life. At times, each of us struggle to make sense of our world and that everyone is on a path of discovery, seeking meaning and success. In general, we all try to make correct decisions daily. However, he added, even with our best of intentions, sometimes we fail. Every person's life decisions are a synthesis of their education, personal beliefs and perception of the world. But at the same time, our decisions are also a testing ground revealing where our loyalties lie and to whom our hearts belong.

Lewis Mumford then quoted Scottish poet Robert Louis Stevenson: "Every heart that has beat strong and cheerfully has left a hopeful impulse behind it in the world, and bettered the tradition of mankind." In doing so he used his uncle as an example of someone who set aside his own personal desires to fulfill his duty. Jakob tended to those less fortunate and in need to better mankind. Lewis Mumford further explained that by marrying a widow and embracing a fatherless child, Jakob had not only sacrificed his personal desire, but in so doing, he had left "a hopeful impulse behind." There were, however, consequences for this noble act.

While the woman Jakob married wasn't his first choice as a mate, she had nonetheless met his deep need for companionship. Following her death, his uncle lost much of life's passion as well as his vigor towards others. Would he have sustained either of his business ventures or his goodwill had she not caused Elvina to be sent away? Or, in hindsight, should he have pursued the young Miss Baron once she was gone? While Lewis believed that no one's life experience should ever be reduced to one broad stroke, he could not help seeing the way Jakob's life gradually and tragically unraveled, rooted in one life decision that brought such regret and pain. Lewis Mumford reflected that no matter the extent of one's success, it was possible, like Jakob, to still feel incomplete.

JAKOB'S STORY AND THE AMERICAN DREAM

Lewis also shared his view of his uncle's legacy and how he personally felt his uncle should be remembered.

Success can be defined a hundred different ways, Lewis reflected. For Jakob Schleicher, success was about caring for others and giving his all in everything he did, while simultaneously taking advantage of every event as a learning experience. As a result of his classical education and upbringing he had plenty of knowledge, but these were only part of what made his uncle unique. Jakob used his heart and loyalty, not logic and knowledge, to make life's toughest decisions. Lewis acknowledged his uncle for being an accomplished businessman whose work ethic transcended his high standards of achievement in every pursuit. For all his passion and dedication, Jakob exacted much of others, but even more of himself. He reinvented himself more than once. Lewis felt this trait his uncle possessed was in itself a teachable characteristic for everyone, as he explained that no one should be afraid to try new adventures. Lewis then pointed out that Jakob had left behind a legacy that was predicated on the people in whom he invested. Jakob left a positive impression with virtually everyone in his life, with perhaps one exception—Lewis's own mother. However, just before Jakob's passing, her opinion of him changed in a positive way.

In summarizing his uncle's legacy Lewis Mumford explained, "Through all the ordeals and disappointments of his life, even the final one, bitterest of all, that the woman he had always loved, my mother, could not bring herself to marry him and sustain him toward the end, fortunately Uncle Jakob had the resources within himself [which] he never permitted to languish."

Today, through distance and time we can look back on the events from Jakob Schleicher's life with insight and perspective.

While some may view him simply as a man who lived 100+ years ago, others may extract a sense of meaning and value from a life that was lived sometimes victoriously and at other times disappointedly. Whichever may be the case, this man's life can nonetheless be seen as both a time capsule from a different period in American history as well as how, even today, it still speaks to the truth of the human experience.

It is clear Jakob's life and circumstances were complicated. There is little debating, however, that as a result of the willingness, the risks, and the courage Jakob Schleicher took in traveling to a foreign land, it resulted in him helping play a key role in America's transition from the steam engine to the now commonly used gas-powered engine. Further, by successfully operating multiple businesses and owning multiple houses, Jakob Schleicher did achieve the American Dream. In finding a measurable amount of success in various ways, Jakob could also be credited for "watering the roots of liberty." However, all did not end well with Jakob Schleicher. For although he honorably chose to fulfill a promise he made to a close friend and marry the woman who wasn't his first choice, this one decision had a lasting effect on him. With the benefit of hindsight, we can now see how his allegiance to his close friend, and to the Fatherland, not only became his undoing, but it clearly changed the course of three people's lives. As a result of this unwavering loyalty, Jakob never attained the one thing he wanted most: the inner peace of having his true soul mate.

Ultimately, every individual will have to decide for themselves what they value most, because at some point their personal and family life will cross paths with material success. Perhaps this is what Lewis Mumford meant when he tried to explain "the fundamental difference between the good life and the 'goods life.'"

JAKOB'S STORY AND THE AMERICAN DREAM

Jakob Schleicher did, however, leave behind his humanness, his principles and his hopeful impulse when he passed away in 1926. Reflecting on his relationships, his integrity and his faithfulness, his legacy continues to speak to us today, bettering the tradition of mankind, one person at a time.

Jakob Schleicher's grave marker. Photo courtesy Scott Mosley.

SELECTED BIBLIOGRAPHY

Allen, Leslie. Liberty: The Statue and the American Dream. New York: Statue of Liberty-Ellis Island Foundation in cooperation with the National Geographic Society, 1985. — Journal of the American Society of Naval Engineers, 13 (1901).

Angel, Ann, Janet McDonnell, and Carolyn K. Washburne. America in the 20th Century, Vol. 1 (1900-1910). North Bellmore, N.Y: Marshall Cavendish, 1995.

Angel, Ann, Janet McDonnell, and Carolyn K. Washburne. *America in the 20th Century, Vol.2 (1910-1919)*. North Bellmore, N.Y: Marshall Cavendish, 1995.

Bartholdi, Frédéric A. *The Statue of Liberty Enlightening the World*. New York: North American Review, 1885.

Billington, David P, and David P. Billington Jr. *Power, Speed, and Form: Engineers and the Making of the Twentieth Century*. Princeton, NJ: Princeton University Press, 2013.

Birky, Alicia K. "Socio-technical transition as a co-evolutionary process: innovation and the role of niche markets in the transition to motor vehicles." Doctoral dissertation, University of Maryland, 2008.

Bogen, F.W. *The German in America, or, Advice and Instruction for German Emigrants in the United States of America: Also, a Reader for Beginners in the English and German Languages.* Boston: B.H. Greene, 1852.

Booth, John. *The Battle of Waterloo, Also of Ligny and Quatre-Bras, Described by the Series of Accounts Published by Authority, with Circumstantial Details: By a Near Observer. Also Important Particulars, Communicated by Staff, and Regimental Officers, Serving in Different Parts of the Field, with Every Connected Official Document; Forming an Historical Record of the Campaign in the Netherlands, 1815. to Which Is Added a Register of the Names of the Officers.* London: J. Booth etc, 1817.

Brailmont, Alexis H, George R. Gleig, and Arthur W. Wellington. *The Life of Arthur First Duke of Wellington, Partly from the French of M. Brialmont, Partly from Original Documents.* by the Rev. G.R. Gleig. [condensed and Translated from Brialmont's "Histoire Du Duc De Wellington." with Maps, and a Portrait.]. Pl. 16. Longman & Co: London, 1862.

Brandle & Smith Company, a Corporation v. the Philadelphia Caramel Company, a Corporation. Case File #1140 National Archives at New York. The United States District Court for the District of New Jersey. 1 Mar. 1916. File containing 306 pages, including various petitions, orders, inventories and auction catalog. Case file dates Mar. 1, 1916-March 11, 1931.

Buschmann, Walter. *Rheinische Industriekultur.* Accessed August 27, 2015. http://www.rheinische-industriekultur.de/objekte/koeln/Gasmotorenfabrik_Deutz/gasmotorenfabrik_deutz.html

Camden, New Jersey, Leader in Industry. Camden, N.J: Sinnickson Chew & Sons, 1915.

Campbell, Ballard C. *The Human Tradition in the Gilded Age and Progressive Era.* Wilmington, DE: SR Books, 2000.

The Candy Making Industry in Philadelphia. Philadelphia Chamber of Commerce Educational Committee, 1917.

http://hdl.handle.net/2027/loc.ark:/13960/t58d0dk2b

Chronik des Langenschen Familienverband e.V. Köln: Germany, 1939

Clark, Judith F. *America's Gilded Age: An Eyewitness History.* New York: Facts on File, 1992.

Clinton, Catherine. *The Other Civil War: American Women in the Nineteenth Century.* New York: Hill and Wang, 1984.

Commercial America, Vol. 26. Philadelphia Commercial Museum, 1929.

Constitutional Rights Foundation. "The Code Napoleon." Spring 1999. Accessed April 2014. http://www.crf-usa.org/bill-of-rights-in-action/bria-15-2-a-the-code-napoleon

Cummins, C L. *Internal Fire.* Lake Oswego, OR: Carnot Press, 1976.

DeLong, J. Bradford. *Slouching Towards Utopia?: The Economic History of the Twentieth Century.* New York: Basic Books, 2011.

Ebeling, James. Letter to Lewis Mumford. 6 Sept. 1972.

Electrical World 16 (July 5-12, 1890); 23

Epstein, Julia. *The Iron Pen: Frances Burney and the Politics of Women's Writing.* Madison, WI: University of Wisconsin Press, 1989.

Exhibition Facts. Free Library of Philadelphia Centennial Exhibition Digital Collection. Accessed April 2014. http://libwww.library.phila.gov/CenCol/exhibitionfax.htm

Field, Isobel. *Robert Louis Stevenson.* New York: C. Scribner's Sons, 1911.

Gas Age, 13 (1895): 198, 224, 282. https://goo.gl/U7eMMs

"Going UP! Sugar Prices Soaring." *Evening Public Ledger* 10 Feb. 1917: A1+

Grant, R G. *Why Did World War I Happen?* New York: Gareth Stevens, 2011.

Grant, R.G. *World War I.* Farmington Hills, MI: Lucent Books, 2005.

Grenning, Wayne S. *Flame Ignition*: Coolspring, Pa: Coolspring Power Museum, 2015.

History and Industrialization of Camden, New Jersey. Accessed January 2014. http://www.ci.camden.nj.us/history/

History of World War I. New York: Marshall Cavendish, 2002.

Horowitz, Roger, and Arwen Mohun. *His and Hers: Gender, Consumption, and Technology.* Charlottesville: University Virginia Press, 1998.

The International Confectioner 23 (January 1914): 8+.

The International Confectioner 23 (September 1914): 39.

The International Confectioner 25 (March 1916): 37-9.

Kawash, Samira "Comeback Caramel." *Gastronomica The Journal of Critical Food Studies.* Accessed August 2013. http://www.gastronomica.org/comeback-caramel/

Khan, Yasmin Sabina. *Enlightening the World: The Creation of the Statue of Liberty.* Ithaca, NY: Cornell University Press, 2010.

Klooster, John W. *Icons of Invention: The Makers of the Modern World from Gutenberg to Gates.* Santa Barbara, CA: Greenwood Press, 2009.

Kochan, Sandra. *The Great Gatsby and the American Dream.* München, Germany: GRIN Verlag, 2007.

Koerner, B. and K. Fix. *Eifeler Geschlechterbuch 1 (Deutsches Geschlechterbuch 99),* Goerlitz 1938, p. 375-496

Krasner, Barbara D. "Lady Liberty." *History: The History Channel Magazine.* July/August 2008.

Langen, Hermann. *Kinder des Stammvaters.* Accessed March 3, 2014. http://www.langenscherfamilienverband.de/?page_id=18

Lawson, Dennis T. *Centennial Exhibition of 1876.* (Historic Pennsylvania Leaflets: No. 30). Harrisburg, PA: Pennsylvania Historical and Museum Commission. Accessed April 2014. https://archive.org/

Levin, Judy. "From Poisonous Sweets to Heavenly Halvah: Notes on the History of Candy." March 9, 2012. *Tenement Museum Blog.* http://tenement-museum.blogspot.com/2012/03/from-poisonous-sweets-to-heavenly.html

Lewis, C S. *Surprised by Joy: The Shape of My Early Life.* New York: Harcourt, Brace, 1956.

Marmion, Daniel M. *Handbook of U.S. Colorants: Foods, Drugs, Cosmetics, and Medical Devices*. New York: Wiley, 1991.

McCabe, James D. *The Illustrated History of the Centennial Exhibition: Held in Commemoration of the One Hundredth Anniversary of American Independence. with a Full Description of the Great Buildings and All the Objects of Interest Exhibited in Them ... to Which Is Added a Complete Description of the City of Philadelphia*. Philadelphia, PA: National Pub. Co., 1877.

Meyer, G J. *A World Undone: The Story of the Great War, 1914-1918*. New York: Bantam Dell, 2007.

Miller, Donald L. *Lewis Mumford, A Life*. New York: Weidenfeld & Nicolson, 1989.

Mitchell, Wesley C. *History of Prices During the War*. Washington: Government Printing Office, 1920.

Mumford, Lewis. *Sketches From Life: The Autobiography of Lewis Mumford: The Early Years*. New York: The Dial Press, 1982.

Napoleon I, and R M. Johnston. *The Corsican: A Diary of Napoleon's Life in His Own Words*. Boston: Houghton Mifflin, 1910.

New Jersey Department of State. *Corporations of New Jersey: List of Certificates Filed in the Department of State From 1895 to 1899, Inclusive*. Trenton: NJ: The John L. Murphy Publishing Company, 1900.

"The Good Life or 'the Goods Life' – The Thought of Lewis Mumford." Accessed May 2016. http://wp.me/p38S12-rK

The New "Otto" Gas Engine. Chicago: S.D. Childs & Co., 1884.

Northcott, Chad A. *The Statue of Liberty and Freemasonry*. London, UK: The Educational & Development Materials Subcommittee, 2011.

O'Donnell, Edward. "Lady Liberty Had Something Else in Mind." October 28, 2012. *In The Past Lane* http://inthepastlane.com/tag/lady-liberty/

"Otto 10HP Engine." August 8-10, 2013. Mecum Auctions. https://www.mecum.com/lot-detail.cfm?lot_id=GF0813-161750

Pennsylvania Department of Factory Inspection. *Annual Report of the Chief Factory Inspector for the Year 1901*. State Printer, 1902.

Peters, Thomas. *Magazine of the Association of German Engineers*. Berlin: Self- Publishing of the Association, 1901.

"Philadelphia Caramel Advertisement." Confectioners Journal, 1902.

Philadelphia Inquirer Classified Advertisement *July 27, 1900, March 30, 1905 and June 15, 1905*. Accessed January 2008.

Preliminary Report of the Dairy and Food Commissioner. Harrisburg: Printer to the Commonwealth, 1904.

"Progressive Era to New Era, 1900-1929." Accessed September 2013. http://www.loc.gov/teachers/classroommaterials/presentationsandactivities/presentations/timeline/progress/

Purdon, John, and Frank F. Brightly. *A Digest of the Laws of Pennsylvania: From One Thousand Eight Hundred and Eighty Three to One Thousand Eight Hundred and Ninety-One*. Philadelphia: Kay and Brother, 1891.

Reinisch, Leo and Adolf W. Schleicher. *Dr A.W. Schleichers Somali-Texte*. Vienna, Austria: Hölder, 1900.

The Remarkable 20th Century. Hosted by Howard K. Smith. North Hollywood, CA: Passport Video, 2004.

Richard, John. "The Columbian Auto Engine." *Industry: A Magazine Devoted to Science, Engineering, and the Mechanic Arts, Especially on the Pacific Coast*. January 1894: 175-6.

Rugoff, Milton. *America's Gilded Age: Personalities in an Era of Extravagance and Change, 1850-1890*. New York: Holt, 1989.

Sass, Friedrich. *Geschichte Des Deutschen Verbrennungsmotorenbaues, Von 1860 Bis 1918*. Berlin: Springer, 1962.

Schleicher, Jakob. *A European Boyhood*.

Scientific American 1 (1876): 339 Accessed November 2015. https://babel.hathitrust.org/cgi/pt?id=coo.31924016244869;view=1up;seq=11

Scientific American 39 (1879): 386 Accessed November 2015. https://goo.gl/5re9Hf

Scientific American 40 (1879): 203 Accessed November 2015. https://goo.gl/1HR9e8

Stevens Indicator. 1 (1884): 46.

Swidenbank, David. "Food Shortages During World War I." March 2, 2014. http://www.porthcawlandthegreatwar.com/davids-blog/food-shortages-during-world-war-one

Taylor, Frank H. *The City of Philadelphia As It Appears in the Year 1894: A Compilation of Facts Supplied by Distinguished Citizens for the Information of Business Men, Travelers, and the World at Large*. Philadelphia: G.S. Harris & Sons, 1894.

Tepper, Michael. *New World Immigrants: A Consolidation of Ship Passenger Lists and Associated Data from Periodical Literature*. Baltimore: Genealogical Pub. Co, 1979.

Twain, Mark, and Charles D. Warner. *The Gilded Age: A Tale of Today*. New York: Trident Press, 1964. Originally published 1873.

"The Two Sisters." *Statue of Liberty National Monument: History of Statue of Liberty*. Accessed January 2014. http://www.ohranger.com/statue-liberty/history-statue-liberty

United States Woman's Bureau, Ethel Lombard Best, Mildred J. Gordon. *Wages of Candymakers in Philadelphia in 1919*, U.S. Bureau of Labor Statistics, 1919.

Varon, Erik. *Sweet Recollections: The Story of the Philadelphia Caramel Company of Camden, New Jersey*. Ohio: 48Hrbooks, 2009.

Weidner, Dennis M. "World War I: United States Food Administration," *Children in History*. Accessed July 19, 2013. http://histclo.com/essay/war/ww1/cou/us/food/w1cus-usfa.html

Weightman, Gavin. *The Industrial Revolutionaries: The Making of the Modern World 1776-1914*. New York: Grove Press, 2007.

Wilcox, John P. *Three Idle Strokes Part I*. Brookville, PA: McMurry Printing Company, 1991.

Wilcox, John P. *Three Idle Strokes Part II*. Brookville, PA: McMurry Printing Company, 1992.

World War 1 in Color. Directed by John Martin II. Burbank, CA: Capital Entertainment Enterprises, 2005. DVD.

ABOUT THE AUTHOR

Combining his interests in the fields of genealogy research and late nineteenth century United States history, author Erik Varon used his love of writing to pen immigrant Jakob Schleicher's life story. Erik, who is a native of Southern California, is married and a stay-at-home father of two. In addition to the aforementioned interests, Erik also enjoys watching sports, reading and volunteering his time in his community and church.

www.ingramcontent.com/pod-product-compliance
Lightning Source LLC
Chambersburg PA
CBHW050535300426
44113CB00012B/2102

> "A very rewarding and emotional read..."
> —Wayne Grenning, Chief Engineer, Coolspring Power Museum

Winter of 1925 brings nothing but trouble and confusion for Belgian immigrant and American entrepreneur Jakob Schleicher. Seventy-four years old and in ill health, he reflects on his fifty years of living in America. Based on true events, *Jakob's Story and the American Dream* weaves myriad moving parts of late nineteenth and early twentieth century U.S. history into this mans' life story.

"Every man's journey is his private literature," author Aldous Huxley once wrote. Reflecting on everything from his youth spent in Antwerp, Belgium to his quest for the American Dream, Jakob Schleicher penned his private literature into a memoir. As you travel back to America's Gilded Age and discover Schleicher and his times, you'll gain insight into the challenges all of us who pursue the American Dream experience.

After all, achieving the American Dream doesn't always result in receiving exactly what we want. Jakob Schleicher's story is just one example of this hard truth.

> "Anyone who has been an immigrant, has known an immigrant, or who has descended from an immigrant will find a great deal to ponder in *Jakob's Story and the American Dream*. Erik Varon weaves a compelling story of how Jakob Schleicher, a Belgian-born youth of German ancestry, was transformed into James Schleicher, an American businessman who dreamed of a world in which art and culture would triumph over national division."
> —Robert Wojtowicz, Ph.D., Dean of the Graduate School and Professor of Art History, Old Dominion University

Maracaibo Publishing
jakobsstory.com
BIOGRAPHY & AUTOBIOGRAPHY/
Historical /Business $15.99

ISBN 9780999055908

PUMPED

CONFIDENCE TECHNIQUES that will have you standing taller in the world

JODIE BRUCE-CLARKE
Includes Free Downloadable Workbook